8 SILVA MIND C... TO MANIFEST YO... ...IFE

Practical Workbook... Kickstart
Your Financial Abundance,
Inner Peace, and Success

Anabelle Alarcon

TABLE OF CONTENTS

IINTRODUCTION

Have you ever wondered why some people seem to be lucky? They seem to have the golden touch and get everything they want in life. Nice clothes, cars, homes, and vacations. Money seems to surround them and everything falls into their lap.

While other people seem to be destined or doomed; life is a roller coaster, permanently heading south. Bills, disasters, health problems, and crises.

Can you relate?

Why does life happen positively for some and negatively for others? Could it be that this is a trap of the mind? Something that is generated from your subconscious, a set of beliefs that hold you trapped. But if that is the case, could your subconscious also positively trap you?

How does your life unfold for you? Does everything go your way? Are you living in plenty and abundance?

My guess is that if you are reading this now, you may be one of those people who's had a tough time. Things don't work out for you no matter how hard you try. And it's not for the sake of not working hard. You work every hour you can.

Perhaps you know deep down, there's a piece of you that's untapped. That you can't reach no matter what you do, that faith will not take you there yet still you know there's more.

Perhaps you're one of those people who are searching for more answers. Because, you know some people have achieved success in wealth and relationships and live a happy, healthy abundant life.

You know deep down that there are incredible possibilities in this life. But you haven't been able to access them yet.

Well, you're correct. So, welcome to your journey of inner strength.

These next pages are going to guide you onto a new path. One you possibly never thought possible. But here you are, which means you're ready. Ready to accept information that previously you may have thought sounded crazy, but now you think the world is crazy and this feels like the truth.

Let me tell you it is.

Have you heard of Helene Hadsell and the amazing winning streak she had over several decades? Her story is unique and it's our nature to think that such luck could be all coincidence. Nevertheless, she had a winning streak that lasted for years. Her story of abundance is well documented, but it wasn't a common one thirty years ago.

However, as we have moved into a more spiritual age; talk of manifestation and abundance is everywhere. Since the pandemic, people seem more enthusiastic to find their life purpose. Knowing that life can be snatched away within moments. And I know there are times in life when you feel stuck. No matter how hard you try, you can't get past your current situation. This often impacts you with a sense of wanting to give up; there's no use in trying anymore.

But yet you see things working out for others.

You may have had a life plagued with self-doubt, limiting beliefs, and negative thoughts. At school, we're not taught how to combat these everyday struggles of life. And we remain fascinated at why success is so hard to achieve.

Very often, a sense of hopelessness can grow inside of you that when you get to your middle years, your sense of time becomes very intense.

Now you are looking for any chance to grow and further yourself as fast as possible.

Maybe you cannot find balance in your life, always lurching from one disaster to another, stuck in a job that you dislike, or in a relationship that's going nowhere. Or on a roller coaster of chaos that you can't seem to control.

Maybe you wake up every day and hear the words in your mind, "I feel overwhelmed. I feel stressed," and you can't seem to get yourself to eat healthy, exercise or treat yourself with the care that you so need to be successful.

Let me tell you that life does not have to be this way. And let me tell you now that reprogramming your subconscious is far easier than you ever imagined. Welcome to the Silva Method!

This workbook will be one of the most useful Silva Method hacks to help you achieve inner calm, financial abundance, and emotional intelligence in a matter of days. After your first practice of meditation in what is known as the alpha state, you will feel a new sense of peace and then there'll be no turning back.

Within the next few chapters, you will have mastered the core foundational skills behind Silva Mind Control and be able to tap into more intuition than you ever thought possible.

And if you activate the best practices for financial success in this book, then you will be on your way to receiving abundance.

Everything in this book centers around personal growth, and once that is activated, your emotional intelligence and self-awareness will increase without you even noticing it. Your success will come in the shape of better relationships with your partner, your colleagues, your children, and everybody around you. Even those who don't particularly like you will be envious of your new mysterious glow.

You will be able to discover greater intimacy with those you love and ways to heal yourself if you're suffering from any health issue.

This book is full of meditation techniques and relaxation depths that you've never been to before. Ones that will guide you to your higher self and greater inner strength.

Once you have finished reading and practicing the steps in this book, your life will never be the same. You cannot unlearn the Silva Method once you've learned it. And you cannot turn off your intuition once it has been expanded.

Perhaps that's the most exciting piece of this journey. It won't take much for you to tap into your greater power, your higher intelligence, and your ability to expand your mind and recreate the life you were destined to live.

Is this the right book for you?

What kind of life do you want to create? You only have to turn to the next page to see how it all begins.

CHAPTER 1: SILVA MIND CONTROL: BACKGROUND & HISTORY

One can choose to go back toward safety or forward toward growth. Growth must be chosen again and again; fear must be overcome again and again. –**Abraham Maslow**

The Silva Method is a self-improvement meditation technique developed by José Silva in the 1960s to harness the power of the mind to be successful and improve all aspects of your life. Since 1966, the Silva Method has helped over 12 million people in 110 countries to enhance their mental and physical well-being, using a scientific and time-tested method. The Silva Mind Control Method is a form of meditation that leads to deep relaxation. In this deepened relaxation mediation level, known as the alpha state, as it is referred to in this method, you can access more of your mind than ever before. The method works in the subconscious area of your awareness, using the limitless power of imagery and interconnectedness with the universe to resolve problems and tap into the Law of Attraction. In this space, anything is possible.

Silva Mind Control is used to increase emotional intelligence and self-awareness. The practice opens up the capabilities of your cognition, helping you create better memory recall, speed learning, self-healing, and enabling you to attract abundance.

What we know about Silva Mind Control is that since its development, it's helped many of its students resolve problems, win lotteries, receive financial abundance, and find and locate lost items or memories, among many other things.

The method works on reprogramming your subconscious. Since you were born, socialization, your parents, and the community you grew up in have shaped the way you think. With Mind Control, you can unlearn that programming, and rewrite the narrative that runs on autopilot in your head and controls your every action and thus result.

The story up next is that of Helene Hadsell. It may open your eyes to what is possible when you reshape your behavior, starting in your mind. It is an incredible story of one woman aligning her wishes and desires with action, to go on to receive financial abundance in the form of thousands of winnings. Let's take a closer look.

THE STORY OF HELENE HADSELL

Helene Hadsell was known as "The Contest Queen," since she won almost every contest she entered including free trips around the world, having her house built for her absolutely free, and a countless number of other contests. Although Helene was influenced by the Law of Attraction and many other books she read in that field, she was a pioneer of the Silva Method, worked as a teacher there, and did PR for José Silva, its founder. She used the Silva techniques to help her win contest after contest. She would visualize herself as the winner of the contest and would focus her thoughts and energy on achieving that outcome. Additionally, she would use Silva's techniques to identify and oversee any obstacles that she may have encountered during the contest. She won over 5000 contests that way throughout her life.

The takeaway from Helene's story is that the power of unwavering belief and focused attention is the key to manifesting your dreams and desires.

JOSÉ SILVA AND THE ORIGINS OF MIND CONTROL

José Silva began his journey as a humble radio repairman in Laredo, Texas, and later as an electronics instructor with the United States Army Signal Corps. Despite his career in electronics, Silva always had a keen interest in hypnosis, parapsychology, and the workings of the human mind.

From a young age, José Silva, a Mexican-American, had a keen interest in the power of the human mind. He was fascinated by the work of Jung and Freud among other psychologists, but always felt there were missing pieces to the explanations. While he respected and believed their theories, Silva felt there was more to the story of the human mind.

Being that his self-education couldn't take him far enough, he wanted to test his beliefs and began preparing gentle hypnosis experiments for his children, who were not doing well in school. Captivated by his children's improvement in school and their ability to see, feel, and imagine something outside of their immediate senses, he began to pursue his theory that the mind had untapped capabilities.

And he was right.

After using mild hypnosis on his children to see if they had enhanced psychic, intuitive, and greater learning abilities, what he discovered was incredible. When in deep relaxation, he found his children were more relaxed and as a result greatly increased their learning capacity. Once his circle of family and friends noticed, they began recruiting him to help them with their own children as well. The Silva Method had been born!

It was through this basic testing that the Silva Method took shape and became the famous Silva Mind Control Method. It took him 22 years of consistent testing to prove his theory that the mind has a greater capacity for intellectual learning and memory recollection through the reprogramming of the subconscious. Once in the state of deep relaxation, a mental vision can create positive outcomes that become a positive reality.

It is a fascinating exploration of the subconscious. While science still does not allocate enough time and resources for this research, Silva's findings are undeniable. His test findings prove that Silva Mind Control has helped weight loss, smoking cessation, and lottery winnings, to name just a few.

Silva went on to create and harness a meditative state where not only positive visualization took place, but problem-solving could be initiated. This is at the core of the Silva Method; using your mind and its psychic capacity to solve problems.

The Silva Mind Control Method is a self-help and personal development program to harness the power of the mind to make positive changes. The focus of Silva's method is to access the subconscious to access our untapped potential. This untapped potential can be accessed at the alpha "level," and the doorway to that level lies in meditation exercises and visualization techniques that lead to an alpha state of mind.

The alpha state is a place where deep relaxation takes place, and through that mental unwinding to the core, the subconscious becomes more accessible. In the subconscious, you can begin the reprogramming to achieve better results in just about anything! These include the reprogramming of beliefs, improved learning, and enhanced creativity.

The Silva Method and its practices are widely used and accessible from home, through various applications, books, seminars, and courses; anyone can choose the Silva Method to begin this powerful method of mind control. Now globally accepted and widely practiced, the Silva Method has become a household name in the personal development and growth field of self-development.

From an altered state, you can direct the mind to do what you desire.

Welcome to Silva Mind Control!

THE POWER OF THE SUBCONSCIOUS

Our subconscious mind gets a bit of a negative rap. We view it as something that stores the bad stuff; the stuff that holds you back our memories or trauma that is sometimes too painful to store in our conscious. But how many of us have tapped into it and found that to be true? Could this simply be a myth to control humankind and keep us in negative, self-limiting beliefs? Let's uncover the power of the subconscious mind in detail and see if the truth lies in merely learning to harness it.

Limitless Potential

According to Silva Mind Control, the subconscious mind is vast and limitless, containing all our beliefs, memories, emotions, and abilities. It operates below the level of our conscious awareness but plays a crucial role in shaping our thoughts, actions, and behaviors. What that means, is that if your subconscious has the power to keep you in self-limiting beliefs and making poor choices, it also has the power to keep you in limitless potential and abundance. The subconscious itself isn't biased toward negative or positive behavior, it simply operates on the beliefs we program it with. Exciting news, huh?

Programming and Conditioning

Throughout your life, your subconscious mind has been programmed and conditioned by various experiences, beliefs, and influences; your parents, the place you grew up in, school, and many more. Sometimes, these subconscious beliefs may be limiting or negative, hindering your progress and success. This is the subconscious programmed in the negative. But just imagine if this powerful tool was programmed with positive beliefs and experiences. Even if these experiences were created only in your mind and you had yet to live them. Just as your fears and worries pull you down, positive influences will pick you up. Perception is extremely important, especially when dealing with the subconscious mind, and this perception creates your reality.

Accessing the Alpha State

One of the primary objectives of Silva Mind Control is to access the alpha state, which is a state of deep relaxation where your frequencies are slower. In this state, the conscious mind becomes quieter, allowing easier access to the subconscious. The subconscious is primed through meditation and stillness and becomes a neutral area where creativity takes place. When you are meditating in alpha, you can't bring anger with you, and if you do, you fall out of the meditative alpha state immediately. It takes daily practice to get there, you need to be consistent and persevering, but it is easily achievable for anyone. Take a moment to recall what it feels like to daydream; this is how you'll feel in the alpha state.

Reprogramming Limiting Beliefs

By accessing the alpha state, individuals can bypass the critical faculty of the conscious mind and directly communicate with the subconscious. This provides an opportunity to reprogram limiting beliefs and replace them with positive, empowering thoughts. For most people getting stuck is the glue that holds you in negative thoughts; you don't know how to harness empowering thoughts, you know how to create them but haven't a clue when it comes to maintaining them. And what's even more frustrating is you know that all these limitations are self-imposed. Luckily, you have already committed to making the change as you're here reading this now. This is the first critical step of learning toward the path of transformation.

Visualization and Creative Visualization

Silva Mind Control utilizes visualization techniques to create mental images of desired outcomes and goals. By vividly imagining these scenarios, the subconscious mind becomes more receptive to manifesting these intentions in reality. Up until now, the term manifestation may have just been a buzzword you're kinda fed up of hearing. But why do some manage for it to work for them and to make their dreams a reality? Surely, if they can do it, you can do it too!! Yes, indeed this is true.

Problem-Solving and Intuition

The subconscious mind is also associated with intuition and problem-solving abilities. By accessing the subconscious, individuals may find innovative solutions to challenges and gain insights beyond their conscious understanding. By using this method your sixth sense becomes a problem-solving tool; remember your gut feeling? Or when you have a hunch? This is your sixth sense going to work and you already use it. Just imagine being able to access it on demand.

Self-Healing and Health Improvement

Silva Mind Control believes that the subconscious mind can influence the body's healing processes. By using visualization and positive affirmations, individuals can work on improving their health and well-being. Imagine being able to free yourself from physical pain by being in control of the messages sent to your cells and organs. Imagine being able to activate spontaneous remission of a disease. This isn't just a possibility, it is something you can explore and take control of.

Achieving Goals and Success

By reprogramming the subconscious mind with positive beliefs and goals, individuals can enhance their motivation, focus, and determination to achieve success in various aspects of their life. Consistent repetition and reminders of your goal and how it will feel once you have achieved it will be your driver or your fuel to push you toward your desired outcome.

HARNESSING THE SUBCONSCIOUS MIND

Now that we have proven the power of your subconscious mind, how do you go about harnessing it? First, it's imperative to begin with relaxing your mind. For most people, this can be hard to do, so by following these guidelines, you can achieve this state much faster.

Relaxation Techniques

You can achieve a state of deep relaxation through methods like meditation, progressive muscle relaxation, or deep breathing. This helps calm the conscious mind or nervous system and allows easier access to the subconscious. When you reach this level of relaxation, your mind opens up like a flower enabling you to receive information to fast-track your growth.

Visualization

Another method is to practice creative visualization by vividly imagining your desired outcomes and goals. Engage all your senses to make the mental images more real and compelling to your subconscious. The only way you'll successfully do this is by having a deep desire or longing for the change you want to see. Try to tap into what the outcome would feel like and embrace the emotion that comes with it. This will help you get a much clearer picture in your mind of what you want to create and help you achieve your goal a lot quicker.

Positive Affirmations

Use positive affirmations to reprogram your subconscious mind with empowering beliefs. Repeat affirmations related to your goals and self-improvement regularly, with conviction and emotion. The positive affirmations you create should not be generic. make sure that they are specific and realistic for you. Avoid phrases like "I am courageous," while it is a positive statement it's not specific enough to shift energy. Try sentences like, "I am strong enough to face my fears and not have a job to find the job of my dreams." A phrase like this will be far more impactful and memorable. Tailor it to your personality traits, behaviors, and obstacles.

Set Clear Intentions

Clearly define your goals and intentions. The subconscious mind works best when given specific instructions, so be clear about what you want to achieve. This must be something you believe is achievable because your belief will drive this intention; make sure it's tangible.

Mindfulness

Practice mindfulness to become more aware of your thoughts and emotions. By understanding your subconscious patterns, you can begin to identify and change negative thought processes. A new state of self-awareness created by practicing mindfulness will push you toward your next level of emotional intelligence. You'll feel calm, clear, and able to accept a new way of thinking; all of this compounds to make the small changes you need to harness your subconscious power.

Hypnosis and Self-Hypnosis

Consider exploring hypnosis or self-hypnosis techniques to communicate directly with your subconscious mind and instill positive change. This may take some practice but José Silva proved how successful this can be for opening the power of the mind and enhancing learning with his children.

Repetition and Consistency

Repeatedly expose your subconscious mind to the messages you want to internalize. Consistency is key to creating lasting change in your subconscious programming. Small, repeated practices are the best way to do this; turning a routine into a habit. They say it takes at least 21 days to create a habit.

Gratitude and Positive Focus

Cultivate an attitude of gratitude and focus on the positive aspects of your life. This helps shift your subconscious toward a more optimistic outlook. Giving thanks changes your emotional state immediately. Once you see that everything is working for you, not against you, your approach to life radically enriches and expands. As a rule, what you appreciate in your life, will appreciate.

Limit Media and Negative Influences

Be mindful of the media and negative influences you expose yourself to. Surround yourself with positive content and people to reinforce constructive beliefs. Choose to read and engage with people that don't trigger reactive behavior, this keeps you at a low level of energy and frequency. What is easily accessible by staying away from these sources, is a higher level of frequency and a higher vibration that will help you attract more positivity and the things you want in life.

Review Before Sleep

Review your goals, affirmations, or visualizations before going to sleep, or upon first waking up. The subconscious mind is more receptive during the pre-sleep and post-sleep phases. So, this is a powerful time!

Trust the Process

Understand that changes in the subconscious mind may take time and consistency. Be patient and trust in the power of your subconscious to create positive transformations. Many of Silva's followers had negative experiences with mind control, where nothing happened for a while. Some even tried practices of mind control up to 100 times and nothing happened, but then they had a breakthrough. There is no timeline for success, you must trust and believe in the outcome and your results will come! Trust the process.

WRAP-UP AND ACTION STEPS

1. Your mind has untapped, unlimited potential and it doesn't take radical steps to get to your next level.

2. Accessing your subconscious is the key to tapping into your unlimited potential. You can program your subconscious with as many dream-yielding beliefs as you want. Your subconscious doesn't own you, you are in the driver's seat.

3. Your first relaxation meditation not only takes you to the next level but also opens that path to advanced self-awareness.

4. Your very first deep relaxation alpha state can be achieved on day 1 of your learning.

5. Once your subconscious is open, it becomes receptive to psychic and intuitive abilities.

Want to see what else you can do? Let's explore the main core of Silva's Mind Control techniques.

CHAPTER 2: SETTING THE FOUNDATION FOR THE SILVA TECHNIQUES

If there is no struggle there is no progress.
–Frederick Douglass

Perhaps one of the most compelling story of the Silva Method is when José Siva had a dream, a clear vision of two sets of numbers: 3-4-3 and 3-7-3. Thinking it was a phone number or license plate, Silva didn't entertain a lottery number, until his wife asked him to grab liquor if he crossed the border into Mexico that day. During the ride, his accompanying friend suggested they buy a lottery ticket, but the lottery outlet was closed. They ventured on not knowing that the liquor store they would buy the alcohol from, had tickets with the number 3-4-3 on them. As Silva looked for the alcohol, his friend spotted a string of lottery tickets with the numbers, 3-4-3. Silva bought all the tickets—a total of 20 and ended up winning $10,000.

Unbelievable, right?

Yes. But true.

And this was just one of Silva's powerful intuitive experiences that pushed him deeper into his study of the mind and its untapped power.

Experiences from students of Silva's Mind Control method have also had incredible victories. According to Joyful Journey (2023), Dr. O. Carl Simonton, while conducting research pioneer in imagery therapy for cancer, found the following:

> *"Getting Well Again - This best-selling classic by cancer specialist O. Carl Simonton, M.D., profiles the typical 'cancer personality,' and gives step-by-step guidance to help you speed your recovery by using visualization and imagination at the alpha level. Dr. Simonton studied with José Silva and in his keynote address at the Silva Method International Convention he said, 'I would say that (the Silva Method) is the most powerful single tool that I have to offer the patient.'"*

Results or miracles are not limited to José Silva and his team. They are abundant among all his students.

So, the next step is to tap into your dormant power. And it's that unawakened ability that you're going to learn here as we unwrap core Silva techniques. But before we jump straight into any one of the practices, first we have to lay the groundwork. Until now, your mind may have resembled the "drunken monkey" that Silva uses to describe the unguided brain (Silva, 2022). So, to make sure the soil is fertile and ready for planting seeds, let's hunker down and first take a look at the heightened role of visualization.

THE POWERFUL ROLE OF VISUALIZATION AND MEDITATION

A friend said to me recently that she hated meditation because she couldn't quieten her thoughts; what irritated her the most was her boyfriend was able to do it so easily. This shows us the dichotomy we all face when trying to meditate and visualize. For some of us, it's simple. For others, it's not so easy, but what matters is the way you think about meditating.

Meditation isn't just a practice to silence the mind, it's a routine to observe the mind. That can mean the mind can be in any state before meditation;

through the process of observing your thoughts and thinking patterns with regular practice, you begin to see calmness taking shape within you. Ultimately, it's a mindfulness practice to bring self-awareness to your body; it's no more complex than that. So the next time you're mad at yourself for not being still during meditation, remember it's a journey of observation that leads to quietening, and thoughts are part of the process.

With all that being said, let's bring balance back to our thoughts and understand the real benefits of meditation and visualization.

Clarity and Focus

Both meditation and visualization are excellent resources to access to enhance goal clarity and focus. Meditation allows you to be regularly mindful of your plans, giving yourself incremental reminders of why you are reaching for this outcome. Gentle practice compounds the energy you have for your mission. Visualization helps you to get clear on your goal by feeling it in the moment; during visualization, pictures of people, places, and outcomes pop up that you may not have considered. It's a great way to align what you desire while being objective at the same time.

Positive Thoughts and Beliefs

Your positive thought pattern is going to dramatically change when you start meditating as it has the natural process of reducing negative thinking patterns. If you stick with it, you will see a less negative, much clearer presence within you. This drip effect works on self-limiting beliefs and helps reframe all beliefs into more positive ones.

Improves Performance and Confidence

When your self-awareness develops through meditation and visualization, you gain a natural boost in confidence. Your performance is increased by witnessing and feeling the outcome of your goal and supercharging your actions.

Attracts Positive Energy and Opportunity

All this good energy created and collected in meditation and visualization makes you ready to receive. Receiving abundance and beneficial opportunities becomes a breeze as you align with the correct energetical frequency.

Reduces Stress and Anxiety

There is a significant amount of "me time" that you collect from immersing yourself in this daily practice; that alone promotes relaxation and acts as a natural stress and anxiety reducer.

Improves Emotional Regulation and Self-Awareness

Mediation, through the observation of thoughts and images, helps regulate your emotions and understand them better. This kick starts your heightened levels of self-awareness; you are also suddenly less reactive, impulsive, and dismissive. Compassion, gratitude, and empathy begin to increase as clarity on who you are and how you behave becomes clearer; this is your increased self-awareness being activated.

Enhances Concentration and Focus

Another byproduct of this practice is improved attentiveness and enrichment of the skill of being present. Simply through the natural process of concentration, especially when you are inside your visualization, you create an increased capacity for maximizing your attention span and lasering in on what you want to achieve.

Cultivates Empathy and Compassion

When we begin to observe our thoughts objectively during meditation, self-awareness increases, and that spills over into other areas of our lives, especially relationships. By looking at the way you operate, it's easier to see what others are struggling with and this provides a natural boost in sensitivity and care toward other people.

Provides a Clearer Mental Space for Visualization

Imagine a garden full of weeds. Now imagine hiring a gardener to clear all those weeds leaving luscious grass, wildflowers, and empty green spaces for new plants to grow. This is what your mind does after meditation to create the base to build your visualizations. Beautiful, right?

The benefits of meditation and visualization come to us from all angles of life.

SETTING INTENTIONS AND ROUTINES

Setting an intention isn't difficult. It's the easy bit; just think how many times a day we say to ourselves "I want" or "I'm going to..." We are in a never-ending bubble of thoughts that relate to needs. However, being clear on your intention is another matter and usually means you have to discover why you want to do something. Just saying "I want financial freedom" is far less impactful than saying "I want financial freedom to free my mind of worry and pressure, so I can provide for my family." The difference between the two intentions is dramatic and you are far more likely to commit to the second.

So, now you've coupled your intention with a reason or why, you need to create a routine. Now this is where most people fail because, as humans, sticking to a routine takes incredible strength. Not because it's hard or even unenjoyable. It's because we always revert to our emotional home, and whether that's procrastination, pain, past-dwelling, or just feeling off, we take very little action to create another emotional state. That's not your fault, but if you've left your mind unguarded for a while, this is where you have to put up a fight to introduce a new mental home.

Take Tony Robbins, for example. He states he has an ice-plunge bath every single day, not because he enjoys it, but because he's telling his brain that he is in control of his mind (*I'm Not Your Guru*, 2016). If a man can plunge into ice water daily then he is emotionally fit and in control to deal with anything.

So, when you come to set a routine, set it for morning practice or before going to bed, at a time when you won't be disturbed, one you can commit to, completely free from distraction. Reflect on your values and priorities, and then follow the guidelines below to get yourself started:

- Be specific and clear in creating your intention. Begin with just one.

- Write it down to make it believable and tangible, adding your why.

- Visualize yourself achieving the outcome. In particular, feel the emotion of the outcome.

- Set realistic and achievable goals

- Regularly review and adjust your intentions. Short-term, three-monthly goals are the best way to do this as you can measure your progress.

- Set a routine to work toward your Silva Mind Control goals every day, at the same time each day, and make it attractive so you want to do it.

OVERCOMING SELF-DOUBT

Trying to rid yourself of self-doubt, or imposter syndrome, can feel insurmountable. You can do it once successfully and gradually over time; it creeps back in. And it can be a purely emotional response; you can achieve something incredible but if you're not feeling good one day, that self-doubt rears its ugly head. Now, that's normal and everybody experiences it, but you can learn a process to implement when self-doubt pops up and starts a negative script running in your head. Let's explore that.

Let's look at a self-doubt action plan:

1. **Identify the doubt**. Write down the type of situations that trigger self-doubt. You'll begin to see a pattern. This will help you from slipping into negative thoughts when it happens. You'll be more focused on identifying the pattern, rather than getting lost in the thought. Recognizing your triggers can help you reduce them more by being patient and compassionate with yourself when they appear.

2. **Challenge negative thoughts**. When self-doubt creeps in, ask yourself: is this thought related to the present moment or does it look to the past or a bad experience? Find the evidence to support your doubt, and if you can't, then it's attached to something that's no longer happening. This will help you to stop ruining it repeatedly.

3. **Reframe your inner dialogue**. Replace self-critical thoughts with more positive and affirming statements. Start by changing every sentence from "I can't" to "I can" and see how that begins to shape your mind in a different direction. Practice self-encouragement by reminding yourself of past achievements and strengths. Journaling is a great way to implement this.

4. **Set realistic goals**. Break down your goals into smaller, bite-size steps. Celebrate each milestone, treat yourself to something, or go out for a coffee with friends. Whatever you do, use these successes as building blocks to boost your confidence.

5. **Reframe failure**. There is no failure, only opportunities for learning and growth. Understand that everyone faces setbacks and not everything goes the way you planned. However, if you can take what you learned from the experience you get to win, even if your plan doesn't stay on track.

6. **Stop comparing yourself to others**. It's only ever you versus you. Comparisons fuel feelings of inadequacy. So instead reflect on your progress and journey and remember your unique qualities.

7. **Seek supportive relationships**. Surround yourself with positive and supportive people who believe in your abilities. Their encouragement can be a valuable source of motivation.

8. **Practice self-compassion**. Treat yourself with kindness and understanding; take the time to journal what you like about yourself and what you're good at. Acknowledge that everyone has flaws and makes mistakes, and that's a normal part of being human.

9. **Take action despite doubts**. Don't wait for self-doubt to completely disappear before taking action. Take small steps forward, even if you feel uncertain. Action can build confidence.

10. **Use visualization**. Visualize yourself succeeding and feeling confident. This can help create a positive mindset and improve your belief in yourself.

11. **Focus on growth**. Embrace a growth mindset, understanding that your abilities and talents can be developed with effort and practice.

WRAP-UP AND ACTION STEPS

1. The power of visualization and meditation is key for improved self-performance and confidence.

2. The benefits of visualization and meditation include reduced stress and improved emotional regulation.

3. Set your intention with a powerful "why" to supercharge your success.

4. This method can help you overcome self-doubt.

5. Create your own actionable plan to overcome self-doubt.

Now that you have an actionable plan, we can begin to step into the Silva core techniques.

CHAPTER 3: THE CORE SILVA TECHNIQUES

The Silva techniques have many benefits, but above all, this method will allow you to access a new source of energy, and unlimited, untapped resources. While that can seem a little scary at first, it is the doorway to having the life of your dreams!

HOW TO ENTER THE ALPHA RELAXATION STATE

There are 4 states of mind including beta, alpha, theta and delta.

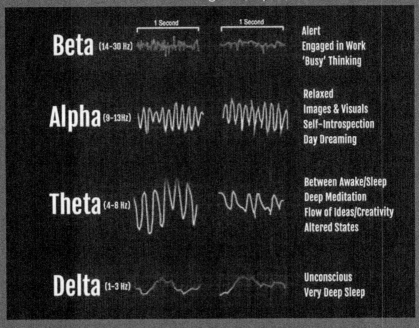

In Silva Mind control we will be mostly concerned with the alpha state. In your present state, you are in beta, best described as your day-to-day thinking. Your first experience of stepping into an alpha relaxed state is not only exciting but incredibly peaceful. Going into alpha is like daydreaming; the place where you get comfortably lost in your thoughts, slightly detaching from your present moment.

Entering alpha is going into a naturally creative state. You may remember back to when you were at school, daydreaming in class time, your mind wandering to thoughts of things you'd love to be doing instead of studying! That is alpha!

Your alpha state isn't difficult to access, it's incredibly easy. However, initially, you can experience difficulty staying there. For example, as Silva tells us, you cannot bring anger with you into alpha, if you do you will pop out of the alpha meditative state.

Alpha is the perfect way to retrieve lost memories. Our minds are amazing vehicles; so much of the time we give our brain little credit, frequently saying phrases like, "I can't remember." If we relax and search our minds a little deeper, all memories can be accessed. Even the ones we believe we have tucked away for good.

Going into an alpha state is not trying to access something new, it is merely a way to reach more of your mind. It allows us to delve into those corners of unused territory, to expand and multiply the capabilities we were born with.

Your First Alpha State

So, now you're ready to gently flow into your first alpha state; let's begin and feel what it's like to drop into a deeper sense of relaxation:

1. When you first do this exercise, do it when you're awake, and set your alarm for fifteen minutes in case you fall asleep.

2. Close your eyes and look up at about a 20-degree angle. The position of your eyes alone will trigger the alpha state.

3. Count backward at 2-second intervals from 100-1.

4. Keep your mind focused on the numbers. You will now be in the alpha state for the first time.

There is not one state of alpha that is the same as someone else's, so don't compare your experience. And do not feel defeated if your mind wanders and you find it hard to focus. New practices take time to adjust to; the key is to not give up and keep consistent with your progress.

Once you're in alpha you may not feel much at all, but with continued practice, you will feel a heightened state of awareness, a transition into deeper relaxed alertness, and a sense that you have taken your first leap into mind control.

Accessing the Alpha State

Accessing your alpha state simply means going to your level of relaxation where all other techniques can be practiced. Being in an alpha state is rather like daydreaming and it will pull you from being in beta brainwaves, your day-to-day level of thinking. It's a very simple way of meditating and it's both fast and easy to do. It is your first stop on your journey into Silva Mind Control. You've done it once before, and here we'll practice this again as a deeper initiation into Silva's mind practices.

So, now that you're here, what can you do? This is where we learn dynamic meditation because here we can problem solve inside a visualization.

The Centering Exercise for Alpha-Level Functioning

This meditation is known as the long relaxation meditation. Its ultimate aim is to bring you to a place of balance and inner harmony. The byproduct of this is huge, with deeper intuition and increased emotional intelligence spanning all corners of your life, including health, wealth, and relationships.

Dynamic Meditation for Relaxation

Dynamic meditation is a relaxation technique often utilized in the context of Silva Mind Control to induce a state of deep relaxation and calmness. It involves a series of physical and mental exercises that aim to release stress and tension from the body and mind. The purpose of Dynamic meditation is to create a tranquil and receptive state of mind, allowing easier access to the subconscious mind.

How to Do the Dynamic Meditation

Dynamic meditation is training your brain for organized dynamic activities. This goes beyond passive mediation and simply relaxing in the alpha state. During dynamic meditation, you learn to sink into a deeper sense of stillness so you can begin to resolve problems. There is nothing passive here, this is your active meditation!

For example, dynamic meditation can be used to help find missing objects. By painting a mental image on your mental screen you can go back to the moment you misplaced the object to find it. This may take some practice but the deeper you go in your relaxed state, the easier it becomes to find the answers you're searching for.

Recalling a memory in beta has little impact. However, when you recall a memory in alpha, it is like living that moment once more, vivid and almost visible. Alpha is like a stepping stone to something bigger, another level, an expanded region of the mind. And the purpose of dynamic meditation is to make an imaginary event real.

The Four Laws of Dynamic Meditation

To facilitate the effectiveness of dynamic meditation there are laws that you must take note of. If you don't, it's unlikely that this type of meditation will work for you.

- **Law 1**. You must desire that the event take place. This is a passive desire.

- **Law 2**. You must believe the event can take place. This, again, is a passive desire.

- **Law 3**. You must expect the event to take place. Now we are stepping into a dynamic desire, one that will get results.

- **Law 4**. You cannot create a problem. The higher intelligence involved in making your wish turn into reality works on the basis that nothing negative, or evil, is involved. You are unable to harm in the alpha state and if you do decide to try this, the desired negative outcome will take effect on you.

To explain this in a little more detail, all evil is activated in beta, so if you try and perpetuate a negative act, the evil will simply turn on you. So, choose a positive solution and learn to accept it. That is where you must start with dynamic meditation. To make all this real, focus on the trilogy of desire, belief, and expectancy.

Dynamic Meditation Steps

Follow the steps one by one, to begin your dynamic meditation journey, it's so simple:

1. Take a deep breath through your nose and exhale through your mouth.

2. Choose a real problem you face, one that hasn't resolved itself yet.

3. Pull up your mental screen. Create the problem on the screen so you can see it.

4. Now gently push this scene off to the right.

5. From the left, slide onto the screen another scene that will take place in the future where everything begins to resolve.

6. Then push this screen off to the right and replace it with another from the left that has your defined, positive, and desired outcome.

7. Immerse yourself in this outcome. See, hear, feel, and embrace the emotion associated with these results. Make it so vivid that it feels real and stay with it make it until you get the full immersion of the sensation.

8. Count down to 5. Now at the count of 5, you will be wide awake and feeling better than before.

Next up is the centering exercise for a far deeper state of relaxation.

Centering Exercise Steps: Deepening at Physical Relaxation Level 3

1. Find a quiet and comfortable space, sit or lie down, and close your eyes to minimize distractions.

2. Take a deep breath through your nose and exhale through your mouth.

3. Focus your mind on the top of your head. You may feel some warmth or even a tingling sensation. Start to let go of any tightness, similar to the feeling of slipping into a warm bath. It's time to feel very relaxed and we will be relaxing more and more as we let go.

4. Now focus your mind on your forehead. Is there any tingling or warmth? Encourage the feeling of being super relaxed in your forehead, let go of any pressure or heaviness. We will be relaxing more and more as we go.

5. Now we're going to release any tightness or pressure around the eyes. Can you feel a vibration or tingling? Let go of any stagnant heaviness. We get deeply relaxed as we go.

6. Now focus on your face, especially your cheeks. Let go of any heaviness or pressure, and relax your muscles. You may feel vibration or tingling. This is good, keep going. We're going deeper and deeper now.

7. Now focus on your neck, especially around your throat. Pay attention to relaxing it. You may feel warmth, tingling, or a vibration. You are now relaxing even deeper, deeper as we go.

8. Staying at the throat, imagine all ligaments completely relaxed. Just let go, getting more and more relaxed each time.

9. Now let's work on the shoulders/ drop your shoulders, and relax them. Feel the pressure and tenseness of them. Feel them slowly relaxing. You are getting more and more relaxed with every breath.

10. Move your awareness down to your chest, and feel how your clothes feel against this area. Relax any pressure, heaviness, or tightness in your chest, getting more and more relaxed as we go.

11. Stay with your chest, and relax all organs, tissues, and cells. Imagine them doing a good job inside your body.

12. Now change your awareness to your abdomen or stomach, notice any tension here. Slowly relax entering a deep sense of relaxation.

13. Stay here and focus on the organs and cells inside your abdomen. Feel the rhythm of your healthy body flow with all other functions, getting more and more relaxed as we go.

14. Now move down to your thighs, and feel them with your clothes against them. Feel your skin tingling underneath the cloth. Relax the weight and heaviness of your thighs, getting more and more relaxed and going deeper as we continue.

15. Feel your thigh bones. Do you feel the vibration yet? You should; relax deeper now.

16. Move your focus now to your knees. Pay attention to the skin covering your knees. Imagine them relaxed, the cells moving through the ligaments. Now they are relaxed, going deeper and deeper.

17. Bring your awareness down to your calves. Feel your skin on your calves, noticing your skin's vibrations. Relax your calves, and feel them melt into a deep state of relaxation.

18. You're going deeper now, to a healthier state of mind. Focus on your toes.

19. To go deeper, focus on your soles.

20. To reach an even deeper and healthier state of mind, focus on the heels of your feet.

21. Now feel your feet as if they are not yours.

22. Now feel your ankles, calves, and knees as if they are not yours, not part of your body.

23. Now feel your thighs, waist, shoulders, arms, and hands as if they are not part of your body.

24. Now you are at a deeper, healthier level of mind than ever before.

25. You are not relaxed at level 3, every time you do this, you will reach a deeper level of relaxation.

Now you've reached level 3 physical relaxation, go on to achieve level 2 mental relaxation.

Centering Exercise Steps: Deepening at Mental Relaxation Level 2

Level 2 is deeper than level 3 and that's where we're headed now. Get ready. At level 2, you will be even more relaxed and when noise bothered you before, it will, in fact, now help you to go deeper. To reach this state, we are going to imagine calm and serene places. Let's go:

1. Imagine you are at the beach, by a river, walking through the mountains, or sitting in the forest. The place of choice is yours, go to your place of perfect peace.

2. Any scene that is passive and tranquil will help you to maintain deep relaxation. Let's begin.

3. You are at the beach. The sun is warm and you can feel the heat on your skin. A gentle breeze touches your face just under your chin, you feel happy, calm, and relaxed. The seagulls are calling in the distance, swooping gently and splashing the ocean as they try to catch a fish. Splish, splash, sounds of the sea in the distance with the waves lapping gently at the shore. The trees sway gently in the breeze.

4. You are now in mental relaxation level 2, where exterior noise cannot distract you.

To Enter Your Center

1. To enter the level 1 relaxation stage, you must visualize the number 1 several times.

2. You have now reached level 1, where you can function from your center.

Deepening Practices

Counting down is a way to reach deeper levels of relaxation. When you first begin, count from 100-1, then from 50-1, 25-1, and lastly, when you are good at getting to a deep level of relaxation quickly, you only need to count from 5-1.

How to Bring Yourself Out of a Level

To simply bring yourself out of any meditative state or level, say "I will slowly come out as I count from 5-1. 1, 2, prepare to open your eyes, 3, 4, open your eyes now, 4, 5, I am wide awake feeling better than before."

When to Practice

There are times when practice is very beneficial for your day. Start with:

1. in the morning, try an extra 5 minutes in bed, using the countdown exercise

2. then at night, this is the next best time to practice before sleeping

3. then at lunchtime, once your lunch is finished.

Start with 5 minutes, then 20 minutes, gradually reaching 15 minutes a time, working your way up to practicing 3 times a day. If you have a health issue you must practice 3 times a day, for fifteen minutes each time.

The Mental Screen Technique

This technique is designed to enhance the clarity and effectiveness of visualization during meditation or problem-solving. It requires you to create a canvas or mental screen in your mind, which effectively you can play with and create images on. But the question is why would you want to do this, and how does it benefit you? Let's go deeper and explore it in more depth.

How to Benefit From the Mental Screen Technique

- Imagine a blank, large mental screen within your mind, like a movie screen or a canvas. This is your mental canvas to project an image on.

- Use your imagination to project mental images, ideas, or scenarios onto the mental screen. This medium is particularly useful for problem-solving, so choose a problem you really care about finding an answer to.

- Make the projected images as vivid and detailed as possible, engaging all your senses to make them feel real. What are the smells, how do you feel, what can you hear and see? Take your time and work through each one of your senses. Pay special attention to your third eye and feelings. What emotions are coming up in this scene?

- Be in control. You have total influence over your mental screen. You can enlarge, shrink, or move the images as you desire.

- Practice making real-time changes to the images on the mental screen, like changing colors or adding elements. You can have fun with it, programming different noises or smells. The most important thing is to make it as vivid as possible.

- You can use the Mental Screen Technique to work through problems and visualize potential solutions. This is its primary use, but you can also use it to work on goals and dreams. its use is very effective for all positive desires.

- Engage in creative visualization, such as visualizing your goals, desires, or positive outcomes. Feel the outcome you desire. Feel it deeply so your brain wants to chase that feeling in real-time, day-to-day.

- Use the mental screen to reinforce positive affirmations or beliefs. Journal a list of affirmations beforehand and be specific about programming yourself with relevant statements. Avoid phrases like "I feel amazing" as they are too generic, try sentences such as "I am strong, and despite my mistakes, I can get through any problem that comes my way."

- This technique helps improve your focus and concentration during meditation or visualization exercises. It stops irrelevant mind chatter and connects you with your hopes and dreams.

- The Mental Screen Technique can also be successfully used to visualize and memorize information. It can also be used to achieve business, financial, or study goals effectively.

- You can utilize the mental screen to reprogram limiting beliefs or negative thought patterns. Again, keep a journal so you can create and reflect on them. It will be fascinating to witness the changes in your personal growth and make you feel accomplished.

- To master the Mental Screen Technique, regular practice is essential. If you are a beginner, try to commit to practicing it at least once a day.

- The Mental Screen Technique can be combined with other Silva Mind Control techniques for better results and deeper states of relaxation. Particularly where health is concerned, make sure you practice at least 3 times a day.

- The technique is applicable in various areas, such as personal development, problem-solving, goal achievement, and self-improvement. It can help you in every corner of life's challenges. You'll be glad you learned it!

Mental Screen Method Steps

This method involves using 3 scenes in your mind for problem-solving. Follow the steps to begin your meditation:

1. **Relax:** Take a deep breathe through your nose and exhale through your mouth.

2. **Identify the problem**: Clearly define the problem you face or challenge that you want to address through the technique.

3. **Scene 1**: In the first mental scene, visualize the current situation or the problem as it currently exists. See it as objectively as possible. Don't miss anything out, feel the pain of the problem, and fully immerse yourself in it.

4. **Scene 2**: In the second mental scene, visualize a positive resolution to the problem. Imagine the ideal outcome or solution you would like to achieve. Don't hold back, see it relived in your desired form, even if you have no idea how to get there.

5. **Scene 3**: In the third mental scene, visualize the necessary steps to transition from scene 1 (the current situation) to scene 2 (the ideal resolution). Picture the actions and changes required to reach the desired outcome. If you don't know the steps, that's okay. Ask higher intelligence to show you the way.

6. **Explore options**: Use the technique to explore different possibilities and alternatives for solving the problem. Be open to creative solutions. Maybe there is more than one way to solve the issue and more than one outcome. Go through all the options.

7. **Enhance visualization**: Make the mental scenes as vivid and detailed as possible, engaging all your senses to make them feel real. This will work best if you can connect with the emotions of all 3 scenes, enabling you to fully immerse yourself in how wonderful your chosen resolution will be.

8. **Positive reinforcement**: Use positive affirmations and intentions to reinforce the desired outcomes in scene 2 and the action steps in scene 3. Write them down and use them whenever you can.

9. **Be flexible**: The 3-scenes technique allows flexibility and adaptation. You can revise the mental scenes as needed to explore different approaches. Don't fear any outcome, simply work through everything your higher power instructs you to.

10. **Trust intuition**: Pay attention to any intuitive insights or ideas that may arise during the visualization process. Even if they seem unbelievable, simply trust the process.

20 Degrees Technique

This technique aims to induce a relaxed state and facilitate access to the alpha level of consciousness. In other words, holding your eyes at 20 degrees helps you to slip into the alpha state more easily.

The alpha brainwave state is associated with enhanced creativity, problem-solving abilities, and improved learning; by using this with visualization exercises you can achieve faster and more potent results.

Like other Silva Mind Control techniques, consistent practice is key to mastering this exercise, and this technique can be particularly useful when practiced before sleep to facilitate a more peaceful and restful night.

And don't forget, this technique can be used in conjunction with other Silva techniques for even better results using Mind Control. Are you ready to have a go?

20 Degrees Technique Steps

To sink into your alpha state, follow the guidelines below and remember to keep practicing regularly:

1. **Preparation**: Find a quiet and comfortable place to sit or lie down with no distractions.

2. **Eyes closed**: Close your eyes to minimize external distractions and sensory input, feeling peace, quiet, and calm.

3. **Breathe:** Take a deep breathe through your nose and then exhale through your mouth.

4. **Gaze direction**: Imagine looking up with your eyes closed at an angle of about 20 degrees.

5. **Mental focus**: Now direct your attention to the spot above your line of sight.

6. **Alpha brainwave frequency**: By looking up at 20 degrees with your eyes closed, your brainwave frequencies naturally slow down, bringing you closer to the alpha state.

7. **Deep relaxation**: This technique promotes relaxation, reducing stress and tension in the body and mind. Total bliss!

Three Fingers Technique

How often do you misplace your keys, feeling sure you can't remember where you put them? It's something that we all do, but this technique is genius in anchoring positive feelings and mental states to access memories easily and for fast recall. Many Silva students learn this technique and use it in exams, at work, and at home. Let's find out how to activate it.

Three Fingers Steps

1. **Put your fingers together**: This is the Three Finger technique. Join the tips of the first and second finger against the thumb of either hand to get your mind to instantly adjust to a deeper level of awareness.

2. **Elicit the state**: Think of a positive mental state you want to anchor (e.g., confidence, relaxation, focus).

3. **Apply touch**: While experiencing the desired state, press the chosen finger gently with your thumb.

4. **Repeat**: Practice this touch association several times while maintaining a positive mental state.

5. **Intensity**: Make the state as vivid and intense as possible during the anchoring process.

6. **Test the anchor**: Test the effectiveness of the anchor by pressing the chosen fingers with your thumb. The positive state should resurface.

Now you can use the anchored touch to access your desired state whenever you need it. The Three Fingers Technique can be used to gain confidence before a presentation, calmness during stressful situations, or focus during studying. You are the master of how and when you use this technique.

WRAP-UP AND ACTION STEPS

1. Learn how to access the alpha state.

2. Try the dynamic meditation for problem-solving.

3. Learn the centering meditation for deeper, more powerful relaxation and results.

4. Use the 3 Mental Screens technique to solve problems.

5. Practice the 20 degrees technique to slip into your alpha state faster.

6. Learn the Three Fingers technique to be able to access mind control at the touch of your fingertips.

CHAPTER 4: MIND CONTROL HACK #1: ACHIEVING FINANCIAL ABUNDANCE

There are two ways of spreading light: To be the candle or the mirror that reflects it. –**Edith Wharton**

It's no secret these days that the law of attraction does work. We hear of countless business owners and millionaires claiming the answer to their financial problems is found in the magnetism of their frequency. You are what you think about and if that's true, and you believe financial abundance is coming your way, it will.

According to Ursula, a student from Joyful Journeys, (2023) her experience of manifesting and abundance happened quickly after taking the Silva Method course:

> "I was traveling on Ryan Air when it was announced that passengers could go for a draw. The winner would win two air flight tickets for Italy; So I decided now and there that I would like to win those tickets and that it was ok for me for it to happen. So I went to my level and programmed for it and guess what??... I was announced to be the lucky winner!!"

So, if there are cases like Ursula's, Helene Hadsell's, and even Silva's winning lottery tickets, what is possible when it comes to attracting winnings and ultimately, achieving financial abundance?

I mean, we don't just want to win, we want to channel direct influence into our finances, right? Right!

SILVA MIND CONTROL'S APPROACH TO FINANCES

The mind control approach works on reciprocity. Money is energy; it's a way of exchanging one thing for another. So, in simple terms, the ability to receive financial abundance depends on how much you give.

Imagine money not as money. Imagine it as a trading tool; forget that it is currency, it's simply a means of exchange.

Then view other means of exchange as money. Instead of throwing things away give them to charity; this type of giving resembles money. It behaves in the same way as money. If you have leftover food give it away, don't throw it away. If you have old clothes, give them to someone that needs them or at the very least, place them in a recycling bin. All of these actions of giving influences your money, and your ability to receive it.

Don't disrespect money, keep a nice purse or wallet, and respect your notes and coins. Pay attention to how you treat money, and not only that; pay attention to the things that cost money and what you do with them. As you increase your respect for yourself through this journey of self-awareness, watch how your increased respect changes toward your body, your eating habits, your spending habits, and the items you own. This all affects your ability to receive abundance.

So, what exactly does Silva's approach to financial abundance help you to do? Let's dive a little deeper:

- Silva Mind Control's approach to finances empowers a positive mindset, and encourages you to visualize, and set goals for financial abundance.

- The mindset shift it creates, cultivates an abundant state of mind and overcomes limiting beliefs about money.

- Visualization helps to program the subconscious to attract wealth and opportunities.

- Goal setting encourages clear financial goals and inspires you to take action steps for success. Unconscious priming of your brain happens and your subconscious pushes you forward to notice things that will get you to your goal faster.

- Stress Reduction is reduced when you have a restored and renewed money mindset, and you begin to have a healthier relationship with money.

- A holistic approach begins to emerge around your finances; it recognizes the mind-body connection and interconnection with overall well-being. This shows up in your finances as self-respect and self-awareness grow.

And the good stuff doesn't end here; you benefit from continuous growth and improvement in all areas of your life. It's no secret that an ongoing practice and mindset transformation lead to financial growth.

Setting Goals and Programming Abundance

Setting goals is simple, and the best way to do this is through journaling. Write down and record your objectives so you can see how close or how far away you are. However, activating them is a different story. Just writing about them isn't enough, although it is the perfect place to start. Visualization is the tool that will help you consciously and unconsciously reach your goals faster. This happens because the brain wants to feel the same feelings you have during a visualization.

When you vividly feel the emotions associated with achieving your goal, you want it so much more. This is the simple tool that helps you take the steps to get there and also attracts the things that will bring about your desired outcome. Here's how you should start:

1. Set clear abundance goals. What is it you want? Be specific. It's okay to not know how to get there, but you need to desire the goal you are setting.

2. Use visualization to imagine and especially to feel abundance. See yourself winning in life. Envision the things you want around you and how you'll be able to help family and friends when you can keep your cup full to the brim, and serve them from your saucer!

3. Engage emotions during visualization. This is critical. Feel, smell, taste, see, and hear the range of emotions that you will go through when you reach your goal. You must celebrate the win in your visualization; celebration gives us limitless joy, tap into that.

4. Repeat and practice consistently—every single day. Repeat, repeat, repeat.

5. Utilize positive affirmations to counter limiting beliefs. Write these down and be specific. Your negative statements about yourself are lies.

6. Practice gratitude for current blessings. Give thanks for everything you currently have and let the universe know that you are living in a thankful state. This will open your heart to receiving and help activate the law of attraction.

7. Practice getting into the alpha brainwave state for subconscious programming.

8. Combine visualization with inspired action. Seize opportunities, learn new things, and take uncomfortable action. This will all push you toward the abundance you are seeking.

9. Trust the process and stay persistent. Some things take time, and this may not but it will depend upon how much time you allocate to meditating and visualizing and then making the required changes both emotionally and spiritually.

Visualization for Wealth

Try following the steps for the visualization of wealth; you must experience the emotions of how being wealthy feels. That will help you to achieve this goal faster and activate the law of attraction.

Define Clear Goals

What is it you want to achieve financially? How does financial freedom look to you? Everybody has a different take on a level of income they would like and feel comfortable with. What are your special or lucky numbers? What number do you want to receive? Write it down, proclaim it to the universe, and focus on that number. What will your financial goals help you to do? See how this abundance affects your life and the lives of everyone around you.

Create Mental Images

Take time to visualize yourself already enjoying the wealth and abundance you desire. What do you look like now? What clothes are you wearing? Who are you working with? Are you still working? Where do you live? What does your new home look like? Make all aspects of your mental screen exciting, inviting, and exactly how you see your best life being lived.

Imagine Vivid Details

Make your visualization as vivid and detailed as possible, engaging all senses. First, look around you and establish where you are, feel the touch of your clothes against your skin, the soft luxury quality of clothes that are investments. Are you surrounded by things that remind you of wealth and abundance? Notice how they feel with feelings of success pouring out of you. Pay attention to your body. Have you taken the time to work out and look after yourself better, now that your abundance has brought you more free time? How do you feel about yourself? What emotion does this bring to mind now that you are successful and prosperous?

Emotional Engagement

Feel the emotions of joy, gratitude, and excitement as if you already have wealth. Watch yourself jumping up and down with sheer elation and love. Imagine spending your wealth on others and feeling how they will feel. Notice the expansion of your heart under these conditions and observe as your light brightens and affects everyone around you.

Consistent Practice

One of the hardest things you may find is sticking to a routine. So, set your alarm for a new wake-up time. Set it again for bedtime practice and commit. You know the benefits of this are huge so make a start and don't beat yourself up if you fall off the horse, just get back on and keep going. Repeat the visualization regularly, preferably daily, to reinforce your subconscious programming.

Create Positive Affirmations

Use affirmations related to wealth and abundance during visualization. For example, "I love to give to others, it makes me feel joy and fills my heart. I love to receive abundance, it helps me to give more to my family and friends." Make them personal and inviting for you.

Trust and Believe

Believe in the effectiveness of visualization and have faith in attracting wealth. It works for others so believe that it will work for you too. And if that feels too unbelievable in the beginning, program that thought into your subconscious, and keep saying it to yourself over and over and over until you really believe it.

Take Inspired Action

Do things you normally wouldn't; if you want massive change, your life will only change if you do things differently. Return the money you owe, stop wasting it on things you don't need, and value the things you have by looking after them well or by giving them to someone who would benefit from them.

Gratitude

Make thankfulness your baseline for everything in life, even the bad stuff! Thank a problem for the wisdom it brought you. Thank an angry person for the opportunity to stay calm in a crisis and say thank you to your bills for the reminder that you need to be a better version of yourself. Change the way you look at everything and watch your world change with it. All of this reinforces a positive mindset, ready to receive.

Use the Alpha-Level State

Aim to achieve a relaxed alpha brainwave state of deep relaxation during visualization to supercharge your subconscious for abundance. This means water the soil in your head and get it ready for planting the most amazing thoughts and desires. A little water each day encourages fertilization of the growth of a new, improved you! Keep it up and keep going.

OVERCOMING LIMITING BELIEFS

Limiting beliefs keeps you stuck, keeps you poor, and keeps you unhappy. We have them due to past trauma, social conditioning, and because we don't make time to retrain our ancient brain that has not evolved alongside us. So, limiting beliefs are a natural part of life. Your brain will always try and keep you safe, use as little energy as possible, and seek pleasure. This is your genetic blueprint which you will have to fight. But to this add in childhood trauma, a toxic relationship, an accident, plus the views and opinions of your parents and society and you have a belief system that doesn't even belong to you. Yet, you act according to that belief system day in, and day out and do nothing about it.

This may present itself as feeling stuck in your current circumstances. It feels like no matter what you do, you can't rid yourself of the same recurring patterns and grow beyond your current level of financial well-being, stress, and success.

Maybe feelings of self-doubt haunt you. You have a negative script in your head with an overall negative thought pattern which makes it difficult to progress no matter how hard you try.

Perhaps you're always stressed, overwhelmed, and unable to balance various aspects of your life which causes immense dissatisfaction when it comes to your current lifestyle.

And of course, maybe you've cut off so many pieces of your personality because you are ashamed to get angry, devastated to feel regret, or avoid social situations because you are often triggered and reactive. All these are normal things that everybody has and need to work through.

But you're probably not in a place where you are ready to face them yet. Many of us aren't.

However, these limiting beliefs are impacting everything in your life, and some days it feels like it's just too much. You can overcome that by reprogramming your brain. You are hard-wired to not always act in your best interest, so the best way to resolve that is to begin working on yourself.

- **Identity-limiting beliefs**: Recognize negative beliefs that hold you back from achieving your goals. Write the limiting belief down, then write an opposing empowering belief.

- **Challenge beliefs**: Question the validity of limiting beliefs and consider evidence to the contrary. Where did this belief come from? How did you learn it? Use the process of reverse engineering to unpick this belief and crush it.

- **Replace with empowering beliefs**: Intentionally replace limiting beliefs with positive and empowering ones. Make them individual and specific to you.

- **Affirmations**: Use positive affirmations to reinforce new empowering beliefs. Write them down, no more than 5 at a time, pin them somewhere you will see them, and say them out loud several times a day.

- **Visualization**: Visualize yourself succeeding and thriving with your new beliefs.

- **Consistent practice**: Continuously reinforce empowering beliefs through daily practice.

- **Advance socially**: Surround yourself with people who are doing better than you. If you are doing the best in your social circle, find others that you can look up to and learn from. Surround yourself with positive and supportive influences.

- **Celebrate progress**: Acknowledge and celebrate your successes in overcoming limiting beliefs. Treat yourself to new clothes, or go for a coffee, whatever celebration mode works for, do it and repeat it each time you have a win however small.

- **Seek support**: Seek guidance from mentors, coaches, or support groups to navigate through challenges. Don't expect to know everything alone, and use this support to reignite your drive and growth.

- **Embrace growth**: Embrace a growth mindset, knowing that beliefs can be changed and improved over time. Don't feel bad when you have to move on from other people or social circles. Don't listen to what anybody else says. Do what you need to do to get further faster.

SILVA METHOD TO ACTIVATE THE LAW OF ATTRACTION

The following meditation was taken from The Alpha Reinforcement Exercise by José Silva, (2011) and advances you into a far-deepened state of relaxation while using the law of attraction. This meditation takes approximately twenty minutes to complete.

Alpha Reinforcement Meditation Steps

1. Take a deep breath through the nose and exhale through the mouth to relax.

2. Mentally visualize and repeat the number 3, three times.

3. Take a deep breath and relax.

4. Mentally visualize and repeat the numbers 2, three times.

5. Take a deep breath and relax.

6. Mentally visualize and repeat the number 1, three times.

7. Now you're at level 1.

8. Now you will enter physical relaxation at level 3.

9. Relax.

10. Relax your scalp.

11. Relax your forehead.

12. Relax your eyes.

13. Relax your face.

14. Relax your throat.

15. Relax your shoulders.

16. Relax your chest on the exterior and in the interior.

17. Relax your abdomen on the exterior and in the interior.

18. Relax your thighs.

19. Relax your knees.

20. Relax your calves.

21. Relax your feet.

22. You are now at a deeper level than before, this is physical relaxation level 3.

23. Every time you visualize the number 3, your body will relax immediately and it will happen more and more as you practice.

24. Now to enter the mental level 2, repeat and visualize the number 2 several times.

25. Now you are at level 2, a deeper level than 3 where noise cannot distract you

26. Noise will help you relax more and more.

27. Now practice visualizing a tranquil and passive scene.

28. To enter the deeper level at level 1, repeat the number 1 and visualize it several times.

29. You are now at level 1, the ideal level.

30. Now do the countdown using the deepening exercise 100-1, 50-1, or 25-1.

31. Choose which number you want to start at and go.

32. When you reach 1, you are at a deeper level of mind.

33. Take a few deep breaths.

34. Now you will go deeper than before. On the count of 3, you will mentally project yourself to your place of relaxation.

35. 1, go deep.

36. 2, going deeper.

37. 3, you are now deep.

38. Affirm the following statements.

39. My increasing mental faculties are for serving humankind better.

40. Every day in every way I'm getting better and better.

41. Positive thoughts give me all the benefits and advantages I desire.

42. I have complete control and dominion over my mind and my other faculties at this level.

43. Now affirm preventative statements for more abundance.

44. I will never learn to develop thoughts of lack or poverty.

45. I will never learn to develop abundance blocks.

46. I will never learn to develop blocks for receiving.

47. I will never learn to self-sabotage about new opportunities that might bring me money.

48. I will never create an unbalance with money and will generously give and receive.

49. I will always maintain a perfectly healthy relationship with money.

50. I am now able to attune my intelligence by developing my sensing faculties and to project them to any point or place on this planet to be aware of any actions taking place if it is necessary and beneficial for the abundance of humanity.

51. I am able to attune my intelligence by developing my sensing faculties and to project them to any point or place within the solar system, within the galaxy, and any galaxy within the universe, and to be aware of any action taking place if this is necessary and beneficial for humanity's abundance.

52. I am able to attune my intelligence by developing my sensing faculties and to project them to the different matter kingdoms, the inanimate matter kingdom, plant life, animal life, and reproductive intelligence, the human body and the mind kingdom, all its levels and depths.

53. I am now able to detect any lack of abundance in any kingdom, any level or depth if this is necessary and beneficial for humanity.

54. I am now able to apply corrective measures and bring back to normalcy the lack of abundance found within any kingdom, any level, any depth if this is necessary and beneficial for humanity.

55. Negative thoughts and negative suggestions about money and/ or abundance do not influence me at any level of the mind.

56. Every time you function at the level of the mind you will receive enhanced abundance.

57. You may use these levels of the mind to help yourself receive enhanced abundance.

58. You may use these levels of the mind to help your loved ones receive enhanced abundance.

59. You may use these levels of the mind to help any other human being receive enhanced abundance.

60. You will never use this point of reference to harm another human being. If this is your intention, you will not be able to function at this level of the mind.

61. You will always use these levels of the mind in a constructive, creative manner for all that is good, honest, pure, and positive.

62. You will continue to strive to take part in constructive and creative activities to make this a better world to live in so that when we move on we shall have left behind a better world for those who follow.

63. You are a superior human being and have greater compassion and understanding with others.

64. Let's count from 1-5, and on 5 you will be wide awake and feeling better than before.

65. No lack of abundance functions at this level of the mind.

66. 1, 2, coming out slowly.

67. 3, waking slowly, feeling better than before.

68. 4, even more awake feeling good.

69. 5, eyes open, wide awake, feeling better than before.

WRAP-UP AND ACTION STEPS

1. Always use the alpha state reinforcement exercise for the best results with the law of attraction.

2. Remember that to receive you must first, give.

3. Respect everything that has value. Don't throw anything away if someone can benefit from something you have. Then give, give, give.

4. Treat your money with respect and look after it. Don't waste it.

5. Share your wins, including financial ones. The more you share, the more abundance will come back to you.

This is probably one of the most exciting parts of the Silva Method you will learn and to think that it just takes practice and a scheduled meditation to achieve, is really mind-blowing.

CHAPTER 5: MIND CONTROL HACK #2: ENHANCING YOUR HEALTH AND WELL-BEING

You can waste your lives drawing lines. Or you can live your life crossing them. –**Shonda Rhimes**

One of the most amazing things about the Silva Method is that it gets you to focus on a problem head-on. There is no shying away from an issue, you get to create an exact image of the problem every time you go to your level. Now that may seem a little overwhelming, but the upside is it's so freeing. When you see your problem in its true light, you can find a solution. You don't have to know how to get there yet, but just seeing the problem resolved is all you need to begin to enhance your health and well-being.

Carolyn Deal (2022) explains the power of helping using the Mind Mirror, another term for the visualization technique explained to us by Silva. She worked with people who had cancers and other life-threatening illnesses but never tried it herself until she found a breast tumor. Two weeks before her operation, she hadn't tried the healing method, but as the day drew closer, panic set in and she started to visualize white blood cells feeding the abnormal cells and creating healthy tissue. After two weeks had passed and on preparing for the operation, her doctor could not find the tumor in her breast examination. The tumor had gone. This is the power of visualization.

Carolyn is not alone, many just like her have used this technique to heal themselves.

IMPACTS OF SILVA MIND CONTROL ON PHYSICAL AND MENTAL HEALTH

So, if the mind believes that the body is healthy, the body becomes healthy, and if we break this down into smaller chunks, we can see exactly how it works:

- Silva Mind Control positively impacts physical and mental health as it combines mental clarity with emotional well-being and stress reduction.

- It reduces stress and anxiety through a combination of positive affirmations with powerful meditation.

- It improves mental clarity and focus through problem-solving skills and concentration.

- It enhances emotional balance and self-confidence through positive affirmations and meditations which induce resilience and a more positive outlook.

- It promotes better sleep and immune system function through better breathing regulation, reduces stress, and supports immune health through lessened stress levels.

- The method offers coping strategies and pain management techniques through powerful visualization.

- It fosters an overall positive mindset and holistic well-being through emotional balance combined with a sense of purpose.

REDUCING STRESS AND PROMOTING RELAXATION WITH SILVA TECHNIQUES

The techniques developed by Silva all have profound effects on the whole body. While you spend time programming your mind for mental change, the physical benefits come as a byproduct of this deep relaxation. Let's explore the specific areas that will enhance your overall subconscious and well-being.

Deep Breathing

Use slow, deep breaths to induce relaxation. We rarely take the time to breathe deeply which we should as this practice boosts our immune system, reduces stress and anxiety, and improves sleep and mental clarity. All the things that are essential to function normally in life. Always take a deep breath through your nose (4 seconds), hold it (4 seconds) and then exhale through your mouth (4 seconds).

Alpha-Level Functioning

Achieve the alpha brainwave state for reduced stress. This is the optimum state for using the law of attraction too; anything is possible from this connection.

Centering Exercise

Find inner calm during stressful situations with the centering exercise. Focusing on your body is a perfect way to feel where you are holding stress. Has anyone ever told you to stop resting your tongue at the roof of your mouth, as you are clenching your jaw? Maybe not, but as you read this, did you feel your tongue drop down and your jaw immediately relax? Knowing where stress lies is the key to resolving issues we hold on to.

Mental Screen

Use your mental screen to visualize peaceful scenes for relaxation. This takes you to a happy place and this practice brings so much joy and fosters a positive mindset and outlook.

3 Scenes Technique

Use the 3 Scenes Technique to find solutions to stressors and ease tension. Stop worrying so much when you can access your higher intelligence and search for the answers. They may not come straight away but they will come.

Positive Affirmations

Repeat calming statements. Combined with other practices they are so impactful at improving your state of mind, especially when said at the deep relaxation level 1.

Gratitude Practice

Shift your focus to the positive aspects of your life. This will enhance your mindset and as a result, your relationship with the world and everything in it.

Progressive Muscle Relaxation

Release physical tension. Be aware of your body and how it feels. This is so beneficial as you start to move away from thinking thoughts and begin to feel your thoughts inside your body. Don't forget, that your stomach and heart also have neurons, just like your brain. Remember, that gut feeling we've talked about? Learning to physically feel into a thought is much more beneficial than simply thinking over it; your body will tell you so much more.

Mindfulness

Stay present to reduce stress. You'll enjoy life more, you'll enjoy others more, and you'll be a fun and engaging person to be around.

Visualization for Relaxation

Imagine a tranquil environment. Go to your happy place and spend time there. You may be in a place of fantasy, but the feelings you generate are completely real.

Consistent Practice

Make these techniques a regular part of your routine. Just having a self-care routine including these Silva practices help induce self-love and appreciation, and works to expand your emotional intelligence without you even trying!

THE POWER OF VISUALIZATION FOR MAINTAINING WELL-BEING

Mental images can be potent tools for your overall wellness but are also excellent for helping you achieve your goals. Let's break down the positive pieces of visualization to understand their benefits for well-being in more depth:

- Visualization fosters a positive mindset and reduces stress, enabling a positive outlook on life.

- It helps manage emotions and promotes balance, moving you toward emotional regulation.

- Mental images aid in achieving goals by helping you go further, faster.

- Improved focus becomes your new norm, as do sharpened concentration and decision-making.

- Your mind-body connection is strengthened and the link between mind and body deepens to enhance better understanding.

- Coping skills improve and you find you have better tools to cope with challenges.

- Motivation increases keeping you inspired and positive in pursuing and advancing your well-being.

- You build resilience in handling life's ups and downs, and others who see this are empowered by this quality.

- Visualization supports holistic health; the connection with yourself affects every part of your life, be it physical, mental, or emotional.

- Relaxation increases, easing tension and instilling feelings of fulfillment as you move closer to your life purpose.

- It empowers you to take charge of your well-being.

- It cultivates an optimistic outlook on life.

- Visualization helps you to grow. Once you've discovered its power, you'll never look back. You'll always know another advanced way of dealing with problems.

UNLOCKING MIND-BODY CONNECTION FOR OPTIMAL HEALTH

Even with scientists now acknowledging that our thoughts have an impact on our physical health, sometimes it's still hard to believe that we can use the power of positive thinking for healing. But if we can make ourselves sick through negative thoughts, surely we can do the opposite, and heal ourselves with powerful, positive ones.

Unlocking your mind and the power of the subconscious helps our physical state in many ways. Let's jump in and explore:

- The interconnectedness that is created from deep relaxation recognizes the strong link between your mind and body.

- The mind-body connection has a bi-directional Influence; your thoughts affect physical health and vice versa.

- Your mind can trigger a stress response, and stressful thoughts trigger physical responses in the body. Over a prolonged period, these can create illness and disease.

- Our immune system understands the impact of our thoughts. Emotional well-being impacts immune function, and when we are sad or stressed our immune function drops instantly.

- Healing and recovery work faster when a positive mindset is embraced. Good thoughts support healing.

- Mindfulness works for the mind and body. Cultivating awareness of mind-body connection helps you to understand more and feel more.

- Mind-body therapies and practices like meditation support connection where the whole body is used to tap into a deeply relaxed state of mind.

SIX STEPS FOR SELF-HEALING

If you have a health issue or disease, Silva recommends visualizing for fifteen minutes, 3 times a day, for maximum results. Refer back to the techniques in Chapter 3, to retrace the steps how to get from the Beta to the Alpha level. Try the following steps:

1. Start in beta (brain waves from beta to alpha range between 7 and 14 Hz) remind yourself that you are a forgiving and loving person.

2. Leave beta now and access your alpha level, through the centering or alpha meditation. All pain will be left in your beta level.

3. Next, simply talk to yourself about any difficulties you're having but in a positive way. For example, you could say "My back is hurting but after meditation, I will feel better and better, and look forward to the rest of the day."

4. Reinforce a loving state of mind, then present your illness onto a mental screen as it is now.

5. Swipe this screen off to the right and from the left present your illness gone, you fully recovered, free from pain, and in excellent health.

6. Count down from 1-5, saying "Every day, in every way, I'm getting better and better."

The key to using the Six Steps to Health self-healing is to treat yourself with as much love as possible. Remind yourself that your body and its cells are not something bad, especially when a disease like cancer is present. It is important to imagine the cells are sick and getting healthy again.

Studies from Silva have shown that treating yourself in a loving manner is the fastest way to self-healing and many people have used this method to activate spontaneous remission, and have healed themselves from many health problems.

Many doctors in the world advocate keeping a positive healthy mind as the key to overcoming any illness. Not accepting the illness as well is helpful because you're programming your mind in a healthy way.

You can do the self-healing exercise as often as you want, and if you find you have pain that won't go away, then use the Three Fingers Technique to get quickly into alpha, and do the meditation steps again.

There is no right or wrong way to activate self-healing. The most important thing is to treat your body in a loving way.

Always reinforce that with positive actions such as eating clean and as healthily as possible and drinking lots of water. Self-care has to be paramount when you're fighting illness or disease.

Don't use this as a substitute for your doctor's advice. Use it in conjunction with your healthcare professional. But be assured that psychic healing has no negative effects.

So any meditation that you do will always be helpful. To get you back to the healthy, vigorous, state that your body should be in.

WRAP-UP AND ACTION STEPS

1. Refer back to the techniques in Chapter 3 to retrace the steps to get from the beta to the alpha level, to practice self healing. During meditation on your mental screen, see any ailments, sickness, or disease as completely healed. Silva recommends self-healing for fifteen minutes, 3 times a day.

2. Creating a deeper connection with your body will free up your mind from negative thinking. Your body will start to feel into answers instead and achieve greater levels of understanding and intuition.

3. Your mind is your body, your body is your mind, love and respect both for optimum well-being and healing.

4. Use the physical relaxation level 3 meditation referred to in Chapter 3 for deep relaxation of your muscles and bodily systems.

5. Remember, anything is possible with healing. If you can make yourself sick, you can also make yourself well again.

CHAPTER 6:
MIND CONTROL HACK #3:
UNLOCKING BETTER SLEEP

Be patient with yourself. You are growing stronger every day. The weight of the world will become lighter…and you will begin to shine brighter. Don't give up. **–Robert Tew**

Some people dream of getting a good night's sleep, while others fall into the land of slumber at the drop of a hat. Good sleep can be life-changing; bad sleep can be destructive; there doesn't seem to be any middle ground, each has a huge impact on your life. But can sleep really lead to success? And if it does, why do we not pay more attention to our nighttime activities?

Perhaps it's because it's just something else we have to do or think about; another task that requires planning and a routine. And that's so hard because we are hard-wired to expend as little energy as possible, that is a function of the brain. So, to get a good night's sleep, we have to go against our nature and fight the brain's motivational triad.

And maybe that's the difference between successful people and unsuccessful people; those that plan and those that don't. Either way— and it doesn't matter who you were yesterday—today we can plan a new way forward and follow some simple steps to make sleep really work for you using the Silva Method.

HOW SLEEP LEADS TO SUCCESS

Have you ever wondered why we celebrate busyness and why we frown on rest? Interesting isn't it? I bet you've never even considered that before. And I'd put money on it that you've never asked yourself that question.

What if I told you the key to success was sleep? Well, that happens to be true and sometimes we have to go back to the drawing board and learn how to sleep all over again. But I know you are going to ask why; everything we do has to make logical sense so we actually commit to it.

Why Quality Sleep Is a Must

Take a look at the impressive reasons why sleep is not only the key to your success but also to looking and feeling great:

- It restores cognitive function and enhances memory, concentration, and problem-solving abilities.

- Quality sleep boosts creativity and fosters innovative thinking and idea generation.

- It improves learning, consolidates knowledge, and enhances learning outcomes.

- Emotional stability increases, reducing stress, and supporting emotional regulation.

- Better physical health can be achieved, it enhances your energy levels and immune function.

- The right amount of sleep helps you to be goal-focused, it increases your attentiveness and productivity towards goals.

- Sleep makes you an effective decision-maker, leading to better choices and fewer errors.

- It generates more adaptability and resilience, and being flexible becomes easier together with a renewed attitude to handle challenges.

- Strong interpersonal skills are enhanced, and you improve communication methods and become better at social interactions.

- Time management is no longer a problem as you begin to respect your time and maximize productivity.

- Quality sleep instills confidence and a positive mindset too, it boosts self-esteem and fosters optimism.

- It improves problem-solving and enhances critical thinking.

- Improved sleep can help you with advancing your career, and increase success in your professional life.

- Overall happiness is restored which contributes to higher levels of satisfaction and overall well-being.

RELAXING AND PREPPING THE MIND FOR SLEEP

So, is there a better way to sleep? What are the secrets to getting a good, restful night's sleep? It begins with relaxing and prepping the mind. Here are a few ideas on how to create the ultimate nighttime routine:

- **Bedtime routine**: Establish a relaxing routine before sleep to reduce stress and create a better sleep pattern that will benefit both your physical and mental health.

- **Limit screen time**: Avoid screens an hour before bed, as the stimulation of blue light causes disruptions to the natural rhythms of your body.

- **Dim lights**: Lower lights to promote melatonin release which will help you feel sleepy.

- **Relaxing activities**: Read, stretch, or take a warm bath to induce a cozy, self-care feeling.

- **Mindfulness or meditation**: Clear your mind and relax, unwind, and de-stress.

- **Deep breathing**: Practice calming breath exercises, as this helps you to feel calm and tells the body that it's time to rest.

- **Limit caffeine**: Avoid stimulants in the evening that are likely to keep you awake.

- **Comfortable sleep environment**: Create a cozy setting that makes you feel relaxed.

- **White noise or relaxing sounds**: Use soothing sounds to block out disruptive noise.

- **Aromatherapy**: Try calming scents like lavender or chamomile which act like a sedative and induce sleep.

- **Journaling**: Write down worries to clear the mind, don't carry the weight of worries in your head, and release yourself of any burden.

- **Progressive muscle relaxation**: Tense and relax muscles for a wonderful night's sleep. Try the centering exercise or use a body scan meditation online.

- **Visualization for sleep**: Imagine a peaceful scene and use the alpha daydreaming state to snooze off.

- **Consistent sleep schedule**: Stick to a routine so your body knows when it's time to relax.

- **Limit fluid intake**: Reduce liquids before bedtime so you don't wake up needing the bathroom.

- **Limit heavy meals**: Avoid heavy meals close to bedtime so your body isn't focused on digestion during the night.

- **Limit napping**: Avoid long or late-afternoon naps as these will interrupt your sleeping pattern.

- **Comfortable clothing**: Wear cozy sleepwear that makes you feel good and snuggly.

- **Avoid stressful activities, emails, and conversations**: Minimize stress before bed, as it acts like a stimulant and keeps you awake.

- **Bedtime affirmations**: Use positive statements to relax your mind and thoughts, preparing you for restful sleep.

- **Limit alcohol**: Avoid excessive alcohol intake, as this is a natural sleep inhibiter.

And if you require the perfect meditation for rest, follow the insomnia meditation.

Insomnia Meditation Steps

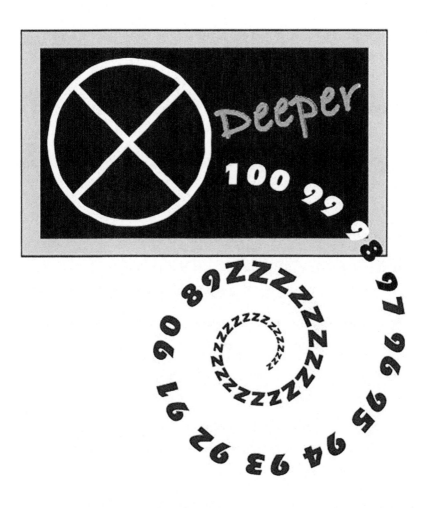

If you can't sleep or keep waking during the night, try the Silva Method to get you back to sleep:

1. Take a deep breath through your nose and exhale through your mouth.

2. Imagine yourself positioned opposite a chalkboard or writing board. Holding a writing tool in one hand and an eraser in the other, approach the board and sketch a sizable circle at its center.

3. Once you've made the big circle on the chalkboard, go ahead and draw a large "X" right inside the circle.

4. Now, gently remove the "X" from inside the circle. Be super careful not to erase the circle itself, not even a tiny bit.

5. After you erase the "X" from within the circle, write outside of the circle, to the right of the circle, the word "deeper."

6. Next, write the giant number "100" right inside the circle. Make it nice and big. Now, take your eraser and gently start erasing the number "100" from inside the circle. Be extra cautious not to erase the circle itself, not even a tiny bit.

7. After you've completely erased the number "100" from inside the circle, move to the right, just outside the circle, and trace over the word "deeper." Each time you do this, you'll find yourself slipping into a deeper, more restful state of mind, moving toward a peaceful and natural sleep.

8. Now, to continue, write the number "99" inside the circle, and erase it just like before. After that, go over the word "deeper" again. Then, write the number "98" and do the same. Keep going with the numbers, erasing and saying "deeper" as you count down until you drift off into sleep.

VISUALIZATION BENEFITS FOR INSOMNIA

There are so many benefits of visualization if you're suffering from a bout of insomnia. Insomnia usually takes hold and leads your mind to stressful thoughts and feelings combined with the irritation of not being able to get back to sleep. What visualization does, is shift those thoughts, and replace them with a happier scene, promoting relaxation, positive concepts, and peace within your body; the elements required for a restful night's sleep. Take a look at some of the other benefits too:

- The calming of the nervous system and visualization induce relaxation, reducing stress for better sleep.

- It shifts focus, visualization distracts from sleeplessness-related thoughts.

- Visualization promotes positive sleep associations, it creates a conditioned response to sleep cues.

- It enhances sleep quality, it leads to deeper, more restful sleep.

- Visualization reduces sleep-onset anxiety, it combat disquiet, easing the transition to sleep.

- It builds sleep confidence and boosts belief in the ability to sleep well.

- Visualization complements relaxation techniques, it works well with other methods for sleep improvement.

NIGHTTIME TECHNIQUES

Progressive Relaxation Routine

Silva's Progressive Relaxation routine is extremely useful in helping you achieve a blissful state of relaxation before sleep. It works systematically throughout your body, releasing tension from one muscle group to another, and creating a substantial sense of calm from head to toe.

Progressive Relaxation Routine Steps

1. Move to a comfortable space, free from distraction. Lie down if possible.

2. Begin to close your eyes while breathing deep into your stomach. Take a deep breath through your nose and exhale through your mouth.

3. Focus on just one part of your body. Imagine it as heavy as possible. Then imagine it as relaxed as possible.

4. Once you've worked on the whole body, from head to toe, imagine yourself in a place of warm serenity, for example, a beach, or by a trickling stream. Feel into this place, and imagine yourself as part of nature.

5. Slowly count down from 100-1, reaching a state of sleepiness on the final number.

Silva Mindful Breathing Routine

Mindful breath is one of the simplest and most effective ways of inducing a relaxed state before sleep. If you think that sleep is challenging, then try this method immediately.

Silva Mindful Breathing Routine Steps

1. Lie down in bed, free from distraction and noise. Close your bedroom door.

2. Focus on your breath and close your eyes.

3. Breathe I for the count of 4, hold your breath for the count of 4, and breathe out to the count of 4.

4. If it helps to imagine breathing in tension and breathing out your worries, do this. Or with every breath, imagine breathing out all your negative thoughts.

5. Focus, as you breathe, on keeping your mind clear and imagining yourself falling into a deep sleep.

Silva Positive Affirmations Routine

The Silva Method promotes the use of positive affirmations, and this can be a very powerful tool in training your brain to welcome sleep in.

Silva Positive Affirmations Routine Steps

1. Find a place free from distraction and noise and lie down.

2. Start breathing deeply, deep into your belly.

3. Begin making positive affirmations such as, "I sleep peacefully each night," "I am ready to drift off into a deep sleep now," and any other affirmations that resonate with you.

4. Imagine on your mental screen, a vision of yourself, sleeping deeply and comfortably, waking fresh and rejuvenated.

5. Continue with affirmations while you gently drift off into sleep.

These nighttime routines can work wonders for your soul, and you can also create one of your own, even combining some of the methods. Always consider what has worked for you previously. For example, reading is a tremendous way to fill your mind with positive thoughts while making your eyes tired and heavy. Don't forget to journal your findings too, this always acts as a point of reflection that you can look back on in the future.

DREAM RECALL

How free we are when we dream. –José Silva

You don't have to wait for dreams to figure things out or wait for premonitions to identify a solution. There is a way you can pre-program dreams so you can find solutions to everyday problems. Using the ideas from the Silva Method you can start planning your dream recall to problem solve.

You are going to recall your dream, your most vivid one, and search it for meaning.

Dream Recall Steps

Use the following steps once your evening, meditation is complete. Write them down if you need to and pin them to a wall where you can read them easily.

1. After meditation, review a problem in your mind that needs reliving. Make sure it is a problem you want to solve.

2. Say out loud, "I want to have a dream that will contain the information that will solve the problem I have in mind."

3. Then say, "I will have such a dream, remember it, and understand it."

4. Sleep with a pen and paper next to your bed so that upon waking you can write down the details of your dream immediately.

Now it's time to go to sleep directly and sink into your subconscious to explore those hidden messages.

Set Yourself Up to Receive Information From a Higher Intelligence

When discussing the process of receiving information from a higher intelligence, it's the same as setting an intention before meditating. It is a preparation tool for your subconscious mind. Think of it as a prepping mechanism.

Recording your dreams is vital because as soon as we slip back into them, we tend to forget them. Use your journal to create affirmations to support your dream recall such as "I am ready to receive wisdom from a higher power in my dreams."

Some like to use an incantation or prayer before sleeping as if to trigger their connection to a higher power or source. Lemon balm tea is also said to be good for inducing dreams.

If you like crystals, then placing amethyst near your bed will also help to open your third eye chakra, encouraging spiritual energy to be awakened.

Using Dreams to Solve Problems

This isn't a practice that will unfold after only dreaming. It may take some practice and repetition to find your flow. And it's also important to remember that your dreams and the symbolism of the things in them, will be very personal to you.

A dream, or part of it may come to you not just as a solution or premonition. One of the most famous stories in The Silva Mind Control Method is that of one of Silva's students. He dreamed about visiting his friends for dinner and was served a plate of raw string beans while everyone else was served delicious hot food. Not knowing what the dream meant he thought little of it, but as he was on his bike one day, just about to accelerate, he saw string beans on the back of a truck. Recalling his dream, he slowed down, and as he tuned a corner his rear wheel skidded. Luckily, he was going so much slower at this point and was safe. But had he been still speeding as he was before, this may have had a very different ending.

That is the power of recalling dreams.

WRAP-UP AND ACTION STEPS

1. Sleep is the key to your success in every area of life.

2. Visualization will make your sleep routines much easier as well.

3. You can pre-program your dreams to help solve problems

4. Dream recall is going to enhance and expand your intuitive abilities.

5. Your mind is the most powerful tool in your body.

Now that you have gained control over successful sleep patterns, anything is possible in the realms of learning and knowledge retention. You have just learned how to make your subconscious work when you are asleep. Imagine what you can do when you are awake! Let's find out.

CHAPTER 7: MIND CONTROL HACK #4: ACCELERATING LEARNING AND KNOWLEDGE RETENTION

Pain, pleasure, and death are no more than a process for existence. The revolutionary struggle in this process is a doorway open to intelligence. **–Frida Kahlo**

In this chapter, we look at several different ways the Silva Method has adapted meditation and the alpha state to enhance learning. This includes triggering systems to access information quickly and visualizations for speedy memory recall.

ENHANCING LEARNING WITH SILVA MIND CONTROL

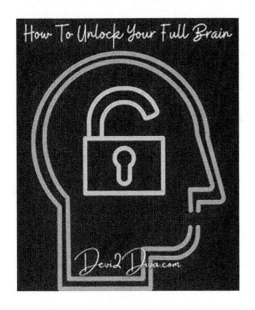

Learning takes on a whole new perspective when you start to use the Silva Mind Control techniques. You'll find learning faster and more effective and will discover ways to access memories instantly.

Silva's learning technique provides us with many benefits, some of which include:

- Enhanced focus.

- Improved memory and recall.

- Reduced stress to enable effective learning.

- A more positive mindset.

- Simulated creativity and problem-solving.

- Clearer learning goals.

- The ability to process information faster.

- Optimized state for learning.

- Enhanced engagement and mindfulness.

- Improved exam performance.

- Supports mental rehearsal and preparation.

- Develop effective study habits.

- Boosts self-confidence in learning.

- Takes into account the mind-body connection for holistic learning.

- Builds mental resilience in learning.

- Encourages lifelong personal growth.

- Adaptable across different subjects.

As you can see—there is a very comprehensive list of benefits. Many of Silva's students have had great success following the enhanced learning techniques. So, what are these techniques? Let's dive in.

TECHNIQUES FOR FOCUS, CONCENTRATION, AND MEMORY

All of the enhanced learning techniques contribute to better focus, concentration, and memory. But the three in particular for speed learning and deep concentration are:

1. **Dynamic Meditation**. Helps to clear the mind, enhances focus, and improves memory. Reconnect with this meditation by following the steps in Chapter 3.

2. **The Mental Screen Technique**. This organizes your thoughts and aids in better concentration. Jump back to Chapter 3 to practice this again.

3. **The Three Fingers Technique**. Revisit Chapter 3.

Three Fingers Technique Steps

According to The Silva Method (2023), this is the Three-Fingers application process:

- Calm your mind first in any situation.

- Take a deep breath and focus your mind on your desired question.

- Now press the middle and index fingers of both your hands with your thumb.

- You have entered the alpha brain wave level.

- Visualize the answer to your question or problem with your intuition.

- Now that you are confident and focused enough to face any test, problem, or question, apply it to experience your desired outcome.

The Three Fingers Technique is very simple to use, can be activated wherever you are, and puts you in an alpha state immediately.

THREE FINGERS TECHNIQUE TO TRIGGER THE ALPHA STATE

Your brain is a complex machine that connects with you through electric pulses; neurons create brain waves, one of which is the alpha brainwave. When you are relaxed you are in the alpha state of mind. The Three Fingers Technique works by triggering the alpha state, which helps you to focus and be creative. Because it is so impactful, you can use it to help you or to supercharge your exam-taking skills exam conditions.

To summarize just how effective the Silva Method is for getting better results, take a look at what you can achieve:

- Enhanced visualization techniques which create a focused and productive state of mind, also help you to learn material for better comprehension and retention.

- Functioning at the alpha level induces a relaxed yet alert state, supporting concentration increase and memory.

- The centering exercise helps center the mind and body through deep relaxation to improve mental clarity.

- The Three Scenes technique accelerates memory recall through visualization and mental rehearsal.

- Mindfulness practice increases present-moment awareness, which improves focus and makes you a student.

- Affirmations for concentration reaffirm your power to concentrate and learn.

- Studying in alpha gives you an edge over your peers by using advanced learning techniques to improve clarity and fast recall.

- Mental rehearsal to practice memory tasks in the mind improves recall.

- Eliminating mental blocks and learning techniques to overcome mental obstacles that hinder focus and memory.

- Mind mapping helps you to organize information visually to aid in memory retention.

- Memory pegs help you to associate information with pre-existing memory anchors.

- Goal-oriented study helps you to set clear learning goals to enhance focus and motivation.

VISUALIZATION FOR COMPREHENSION AND RETENTION

Visualization naturally helps with learning comprehension and retention. The use of creating mental images leads to better understanding and the storytelling you undertake during the practice aids memory and recall. A fun way of making stories unique is to use symbols for complex ideas or associate new information with existing knowledge.

Attach emotions to your visualizations and engage all your senses. Visualize the sequence of events for understanding and review and visualize your learned material.

Combine visualization with reading or listening and create concept maps for the organization. Use multi-sensory elements for deeper learning and utilize guided visualizations and study groups, these are super effective.

Finally, practice mental rehearsal and repetition for reinforcement.

HOW TO CREATE A TRIGGERING MECHANISM

The easiest way to do this and improve your memory is by using the Three Fingers Technique.

1. Put your thumb and first 2 fingers together.

2. Say "Whenever I put these fingers together, I will immediately reach my level."

Instantly, your memory will be triggered to remember important key information. By using the Three Fingers technique you instantly put yourself into an alpha state.

HOW TO IMPROVE YOUR MEMORY USING MEMORY PEGS

When you need to remember many items, you can create a memory recall tactic to help you store and recall information.

1. Write numbers from 1-30.

2. Create symbols for each number. Learn them when in the alpha state.

3. When you need to learn 30 pieces of information, these become memory pegs.

4. Associate each item or piece of information with the symbol from each number.

5. For example, your symbol for number 1 may be the sun, and your piece of information for number 1 may be glasses. Therefore, you would visualize and remember number 1 as sunglasses.

6. Visualize and memorize your memory pegs in alpha first.

7. Then memorize them in beta.

HOW TO USE SPEED LEARNING

These are the steps to activate when you want to learn at a faster pace:

1. Read the chapter or information you need to learn, into a voice recorder while you are in beta.

2. Go to your level, you can use the Three Fingers Technique or count backward to get there.

3. Play back the recording, but if pressing play brings you out of alpha, try and have someone press it for you. Or use the Three Fingers Technique to get back to alpha.

4. Focus deeply on your voice. Listen to your recording.

This is a very effective way of learning that cuts learning time in half and brings out your confidence when you need to recall information, especially under stressful conditions.

WRAP-UP AND ACTION STEPS

1. There are 3 core Silva techniques especially suited to improve speed learning and deep focus and centration including The Dynamic Meditation, the Mental Screen Technique and the Three Fingers Technique.

2. Visualization is a unique tool to help you recall memories and study notes.

3. Learn the Three Fingers Technique to immediately trigger your alpha state for enhanced learning.

4. Create your triggering mechanism under visualization so you can use it in beta.

5. Create a system to use memory pegs to instantly recall lots of information.

6. Practice using speed learning for deeper memory recollection.

7. Refer back to Chapter 3 for a refresher on all the core Silva techniques.

CHAPTER 8: MIND CONTROL HACK #5: TRANSFORMING RELATIONSHIPS AND INTIMACY

Though no one can go back and make a brand new start, anyone can start from now and make a brand new ending.
–Carl Bard

You can transform everything in life, from your mind to your body to your relationships. Nothing has to stay the same. You only need the desire for change and pointers to guide you in a new direction. Are you ready to transform your intimacy levels and watch your relationship bloom?

IMPROVING RELATIONSHIPS AND COMMUNICATION WITH SILVA MIND CONTROL

Using the Silva Method to create deeper levels of intimacy is a fantastic way to enhance your relationship, especially if you and your partner both agree that you want a long-lasting, deeply intimate relationship.

By following this next meditation, you can begin to unwrap deeper levels of connection, and a more profound understanding of each other's needs.

Intimacy Meditation Steps

Here are the meditation steps to follow to achieve this:

1. Select a place where you both feel happy and relaxed. This can be any place where you both have good memories that you share. This place can be one you've never visited before however, you must create this imaginary destination together. You cannot go somewhere that only one of you has visited, as this reduces the sense of sharing and may hurt the purpose of the intimate meditation.

2. Find a place where you won't be disturbed or distracted. Sit close, facing each other, relax, and close your eyes.

3. Breathe Deeply. Then one person says, "I'm going to count slowly from 10-1, and with each count, you will go deeper into a pleasant, meditative state." Then begin counting slowly, pausing between numbers to say, "going deeper and deeper."

4. Start counting backward.

5. Once you reach number 1, say "You are now relaxed at a deep level of mind."

6. Now the other person counts slowly backward from 10-1, to allow the other person to go to the special place. Say "With each count, we'll become closer."

7. The last person counting says "We are now both relaxed at a pleasant level of mind. Let's go deeper together, let's experience our place of relaxation together."

8. Each of you, in turn, will slowly and spontaneously explain the scene you see together, detailing the sights, sounds, smells, and feelings you have.

9. Then one of you will say "I want most in life to make you happy, and only then do I want to make myself happy."

10. The other person repeats it.

11. Stay in this silent communion for as long as you wish. You can gaze into each other's eyes if you wish.

12. Then awaken saying "5, 4, 3, 2, 1, we are wide awake feeling better than before."

Immediately, a sense of deeper significance and a stronger emotional bond will appear in your relationship; and the more you practice this, the deeper it will go. But what does this mean in real terms, in day-to-day communication, and how can we measure its impact to see if it's working?

How the Intimacy Meditation Will Benefit Your Relationship

Be on the lookout for these positive changes in your relationship:

Enhanced Empathy and Understanding

As you begin to share emotions, your confidence will grow in being open and honest with your partner which will increase your emotional connection.

Improved Active Listening

Active listening is when you truly hear what your partner is saying. You are not simply waiting until they've finished for your turn to voice your opinion. This helps build trust. Listening effectively opens the door to more honest and open communication.

Better Emotional Regulation

When you can regulate your emotions your emotional intelligence increases. This is exactly what is needed for a successful and long-lasting relationship. Less reactive and impulsive behavior and less conflict and arguments, the very things that put distance between two people and lead to bitterness and resentment.

Heightened Awareness of Non-Verbal Communication

Have you ever wondered how it feels to know what your partner is thinking or feeling? This is completely achievable when you start to connect with your partner's frequency within their energy field. When two people have different emotions, tied to one another, their energy fields overlap and they begin to think and feel together. This is an incredible place to be with your partner.

Effective Conflict Resolution

When conflict arises from time to time, and it will, that is part of life, you'll find that arguments and disagreements are much easier to resolve. Emotions won't flare up so deeply and you'll be willing to avoid conflict. Seeing your partner's point of view becomes your new way of thinking and your experience of conflict will rapidly change, with you being able to empathize and calmly resolve something that went wrong. Escalated arguments or aggression will become a thing of the past.

Empowerment in Communication

Fear can drive a deep wedge into your relationship; it drives a wedge into any relationship but the difference here is this is probably one of the most important unions you need to protect and nurture. When you are able to say anything to your partner, in your most vulnerable state, there is simply no greater level of intimacy.

Strengthened Trust in Relationships

Trust is the foundation of any relationship and your bond will be most sacred when you continuously strengthen your level of trust. Renewed and enhanced intimacy does this and makes your relationship feel impenetrable.

Mindful and Present-Moment Engagement

Living in a future state of mind can be as damaging as living in the past. If you are not able to be active in the present moment, you cannot enjoy your relationships right now. What this meditation does to enhance this is bring you back to the present moment immediately. Even if you have created a place of fantasy to experience your partner, you are still connected to them in the now. Remembering these moments together also connects you in the same space which ignites the passion and closeness you create together.

Positive Outlook for Better Interactions

Having a negative mindset weighs you down, and reduces your energetical vibration and frequency; it turns you into someone that others don't want to be around. But having a positive outlook completely changes that. Your partner will be more receptive to you, will want to share ideas and thoughts with you, and spend time with you when you have a more positive outlook. And don't forget positivity multiplies when you feel it, it's great for not only your mind but your body too.

Compassionate Communication

Greater intimacy levels will allow you to speak from the heart space. When we are "in our heads" are we speaking from the heart, communicating what we need and want? Or are we trying to please the other person by saying what we think they want to hear? Compassionate communication grows under these levels of intimacy, it also brings the needs of others to the forefront enriching and blessing our relationships.

Addressing Communication Blocks

Your relationships can be transformed when you begin to suppress communication blocks. When you've achieved this elevated level of emotional intelligence you can talk about problems without fear of judgment. Expressing things that bother you negates them and takes the power away from negative influence on your sacred union.

Respecting Boundaries in Relationships

Everybody has boundaries in relationships and this isn't something to be afraid of. We all have experiences that shape our outlook on life and sometimes you or your partner must create boundaries to feel safe. That is okay. But when we don't fully understand and lack self-awareness, it's easy to step over those boundaries, leaving your partner feeling violated or disrespected. This can be completely negated once a deeper level of intimacy is created by using the Silva Method.

Deeper Emotional Intimacy

Enriched emotional closeness is a byproduct of using intimacy meditation. There is nothing like having a greater sense of satisfaction from the fulfillment of your closest bond. Living without fear of jealousy, resentment, affairs, and conflict is a beautiful place to live and one we dream about having in relationships; it's the ultimate peace.

Cultivating Gratitude and Support

Support in both physical activities and in an emotional sense is what two partners need. To know and feel that someone is on your side is the ultimate trust. Being thankful for your partner deepens your love. Appreciation, gratitude, and compassion are possibly the most powerful emotions you can feel, and working on your intimacy levels, greatly strengthens them all.

Enhanced Interpersonal Skills

Who doesn't need a team? Working alone through the adventure of life can feel hugely isolating and lonely, especially when so much of the Western world experiences family-related trauma. Having someone on your side promotes strength and courage and enables you to be someone who helps others too; it has a glorious, ripple effect.

Listening to Understand Others

Listening to others is an exercise in empathy, not in waiting for your turn to speak. How many times have you tried to talk to someone knowing that they are just waiting for you to finish so they can get their point across? It's incredibly frustrating and it doesn't feel good. Listening to understand is a completely different notion. It doesn't require you to speak at all or give your opinion; it simply requires you to hear your partner's thoughts and feelings. It's your choice how you internalize or communicate back if you need to, and what it does do is create elevated levels of understanding.

Assertive Expression of Needs

When you and your partner create greater feelings of intimacy you are both able to be assertive without being forceful or demanding. When one side feels pressured in a relationship, it doesn't feel good and can negatively impact two people. But when you are feeling comfortable and stable enough to say what you need without complaining, nothing is a problem and you feel at ease expressing your needs to your partner.

Clarifying Misunderstandings

Deepened levels of intimacy mean that you can clear up misunderstandings very quickly without them getting confused and translating into further problems. Very often when we have communication errors, we interpret what has happened through our own beliefs, and that can leave out another person's perspective of the issue. But in a state of strengthened understanding that rarely happens, and when it does it is quickly dissolved. The build-up of resentment is so damaging in a relationship, don't let it happen to yours when you can simply spend time working on your intimacy through meditation.

Strengthening Emotional Bonds

Both compassion and care in a relationship make the ultimate union. Emotional bonds are life's creations that empower you and others to achieve your dreams and goals; you don't have to do things alone. It's usually the mental impact of emotional bonds that give you courage and resilience, two things needed to face life's challenges.

Prioritizing Your Relationship

Everybody needs to feel important. Everyone. It is one of the most fundamental, basic human needs and this will significantly develop if you are prioritizing your relationship by taking the time and care to work on it together.

HOW TO RESOLVE CONFLICT AND FOSTER UNDERSTANDING

You will see the transformation of your relationship when you're able to resolve conflict and foster understanding. Using Silva's intimacy method provides a gateway to introducing enhanced levels into your most precious relationship. It won't happen overnight and there will always be different layers of the onion to peel, but here are some helpful guidelines on what to do to relieve conflict and begin to foster understanding:

- **Active listening**: Pay full attention to the other person, demonstrate empathy, and avoid interrupting while they express their concerns. Do not just wait for your turn to speak.

- **Remain calm**: Stay composed and avoid reacting emotionally, as it can escalate the situation further. Be mindful of being impulsive and reactive, both stages which will create more conflict.

- **Identify common ground**: Look for shared interests or goals to establish a basis for finding common ground.

- **Communicate clearly**: Use "I" statements to express your feelings and concerns without blaming or accusing the other person. Repeatedly using "You" makes your partner feel blamed and accused.

- **Find compromise**: Be open to finding a middle ground and be willing to make concessions to resolve an issue, this is where being empathetic really helps.

- **Seek mediation**: If necessary, involve a neutral third party to mediate the conversation and facilitate a constructive dialogue.

- **Focus on solutions**: Shift the focus from dwelling on the problem to brainstorming possible solutions together. This will have a huge impact on you both and remind each other to stay solution-focused.

- **Forgive and let go**: Once a resolution is reached, release any lingering resentment and move forward positively. If you hold on to tatters of negativity it will eat at your relationship and all the positive things you are both working toward.

- **Embrace diversity**: Recognize and appreciate the differences in perspective, background, and experience of others.

- **Practice empathy**: Put yourself in others' shoes to better understand their feelings and reactions. A perfect way to do this is by going on an empathy "walk". Letting the other person speak for 30 minutes or an hour, about how they see their issues, while you remain silent.

- **Ask questions**: Encourage open communication by asking questions to clarify others' viewpoints and intentions. If you're not sure how to do this sensitively, always ask beforehand, "Is it okay if I ask a question?" or "Can I offer my thoughts on this?" And wait for permission before you go ahead.

- **Active engagement**: Be genuinely interested in learning about others and their experiences. You can't fake this, so if it's hard for you then really focus on active listening first.

- **Respectful communication**: Promote a culture of respectful and constructive communication, even when discussing differences.

- **Share personal experiences**: Use storytelling as a way to connect with others and foster understanding. Your mess often becomes your message.

- **Avoid assumptions**: Refrain from making assumptions about others based on stereotypes or limited information. free your mind of unconscious bias and listen to the other person.

- **Educate yourself**: Continuously learn about different cultures, perspectives, and backgrounds to broaden your understanding. By doing this you will think and feel differently, and you will increase your self-awareness and emotional intelligence, which is your greatest asset.

ENHANCING INTIMACY WITH VISUALIZATION

Visualization is a potent tool to act as a gateway to more meaningful experiences, and those are what you deeply desire with your partner! It opens the door to better communication, active listening, and vulnerability in your relationship, the very ingredients you need to make a fulfilling, contented relationship.

Follow this guide for ways to enhance your intimacy through the power of visualization:

1. **Make time for each other in a quiet and comfortable place**. An area free from distraction or noise is very important to set the scene for your intimate mind journey.

2. **Relax both your mind and body**. Usually, if you sit or lie down, this deepens your relaxed state, enabling your experience to go much deeper and feel more enjoyable.

3. **Discuss and set your intentions**. Talk about how you both want more intimacy in your relationship. What does intimacy mean for you both? How does it look? See it from both perspectives, as we all have different needs.

4. **Choose a positive memory to recall, or go to your special place**. Go back to an amazing location where you spent time together, or work on creating one in the future. Close your eyes when you discuss this and feel the ripples of excitement or goosebumps on your skin.

5. **Explore and engage all your senses**. Work through your vision so you can see, hear, smell, and feel everything to enhance your experience, and get closer to each other.

6. **Feel the emotions**. What emotions are you feeling at the time? Share and explore them from both sides and ask each other questions about how those emotions show up in your physical body. See if you can describe the feelings and physical sensations.

7. **Project your ideal outcome into the future**. Now move to a visualization of you both in the future. Imagine scenarios where you can see greater levels of intimacy and a stronger relationship. In particular, pay attention to moments of greater levels of trust, vulnerability, and better communication.

8. **Welcome open communication**. Imagine being able to speak and say anything to each other without conflict or misunderstanding. Embrace new levels of understanding with each other.

9. **Visualize conflict resolution**. See yourself resolving disagreements with love and from the heart space, with oodles of understanding and care.

10. **See physical intimacy**. Create a sense of cuddling, hugging, holding hands, and any other intimate scenes that make you feel close to each other.

11. **Set as a regular practice**. An ideal way to experience intimacy meditation would be as a daily practice, however, that may feel a little too much in the beginning. Initially, set it as a weekly practice and you will quickly see how you want to come back to this deeply relaxed space more frequently as you feel and see the benefits of it.

12. **Apply your visualization to real-life situations**. Use all the positive energy created in your visualization to harness your daily interaction with your partner. Recall them to that space and stay in the same energy. Life often has us snapping back to a less preferable emotion, but you can both remain present to hold each other accountable. Don't do it negatively but also don't be afraid to bring each other back to that blissful space whenever you need to. If you don't know where to start, simply hold your partner's hand or cuddle them saying, "Do you remember the place we went to in our intimacy meditation?" and I guarantee you'll both be back there in your mind in an instant!

WRAP-UP AND ACTION STEPS

1. Greater levels of intimacy can revive a broken relationship.

2. Practice *the Intimacy Meditation* whenever you need to get back into synch with your partner.

3. A deeper understanding of one relationship can help you in all relationships as it creates a ripple effect, leading to enhanced emotional intelligence.

4. You can create the relationship you dream about through intimacy visualization.

5. You can say things you've been scared or too timid to say when you are in a deeply relaxed, vulnerable, shared state with your partner.

6. You can pass on this experience and knowledge to those around you and help them develop closer relationships too.

Wow! I know you're probably feeling excited to try the intimacy meditation as it's nothing less than relationship transforming! And when you couple this with greater levels of spirituality, your sacred alliance with your partner will continue to grow and grow. How do you create deeper levels of spiritual growth? Well, I'm about to share that with you now!

CHAPTER 9: MIND CONTROL HACK #6: SPIRITUAL GROWTH AND INNER HARMONY

First things first might be a cliché, but it's a useful one that means prioritizing what matters most to you and believing there is no wrong answer. –**Stacey Abrams**

Ultimately, your spiritual growth and inner harmony give you a sense of purpose in your life, and this is something that every human being on the planet searches for. A greater sense of purpose leads to increased creativity and a feeling of alignment. Once things are deeply experienced, the universe behaves like a magnet, attracting all that is good and meaningful for you. You begin to live in abundance; and of course, elevated levels of spiritual harmony and wisdom.

Now that sounds like a glorious place to be, so let's find out exactly how to do it.

SPIRITUAL ASPECTS OF SILVA MIND CONTROL

The Silva Mind Control method is not affiliated with any one religion or practice. It focuses on your level of higher intelligence, and you can translate that in any way you want. Some refer to it as Source, Spirit, Christ, or God; there is no right or wrong way, just wherever you feel your faith lies.

You can use the Silva Method easily and without conflict with any type of beliefs, whatever they might be. So, let's break down the spiritual elements of Mind Control, so we can develop a deeper understanding of how we can achieve greater spiritual growth and inner harmony.

The Spiritual Elements Unpacked

The following elements are the spiritual aspects of the mind control practice that you can explore on this incredible journey of expansion:

- **Inner connection**: Silva Mind Control emphasizes connecting with one's inner self and higher consciousness. Inner connection is the best route to abundance and living life on your own terms.

- **Intuition and guidance**: The core practices and techniques of Silva Mind control teach you how to hone your intuition. Practitioners are encouraged to tap into their intuition for spiritual guidance. You will often find the answers you need inside your intuition and this creates the guidance you need to follow. Remember to listen to your gut feelings and your hunches. This is your intuition guiding you. Make use of it. It usually points you in the right direction.

- **Mind-body-spirit harmony**: Silva's techniques promote alignment and balance among mind, body, and spirit. When you are completely aligned the universe matches your unique vibration. Your energetic frequency then elevates and you become a magnet. This is when you see people's lives explode with the most wonderful successes and relationships.

- **Universal energy**: Acknowledges and works with the concept of universal energy or the unified field.

- **Transcendence**: Spiritual growth and transformation are fostered through Silva's practices. This provides greater resilience towards life's challenges and puts goals, and dreams within easier reach.

- **Higher purpose**: Individuals always seek to explore their higher purpose and meaning in life. When you go within yourself on your journey of self-discovery, you unwittingly discover the keys to what aligns you with your higher purpose or mission in this lifetime.

- **Oneness and unity**: Silva promotes a sense of oneness with the universe and all living beings. Oneness with the universe and all that is it increases our interconnectedness and helps us kickstart our journey of transcending our ego. This enables you to live in your truth, and be the authentic person you want to be.

- **Positive affirmations**: Utilize affirmations to reinforce spiritual beliefs and intentions. These help you to manifest and instill the power and positivity to live in harmony with yourself and those around you.

- **Visualization for manifestation**: Visualization is used to manifest spiritual goals and aspirations. It is an extremely useful tool that helps you to create things.

- **Gratitude and appreciation**: Practitioners cultivate gratitude and appreciation for life's blessings. Living in gratitude strengthens your emotional intelligence, an attribute that will get you further in life than any amount of money or qualification.

- **Meditation and mindfulness**: Spiritual aspects involve meditative practices and present-moment awareness. Living in the now is imperative to living a fulfilled life.

- **Spiritual healing**: Silva techniques can be employed for spiritual healing and inner peace. This also spills over into other types of healing; such as healing illness for example. All physical conditions are created by the mind, so can also be healed by the mind as well.

- **Expanded consciousness**: Silva Mind Control may lead to expanded states of consciousness, which in turn leads to greater creativity and increased life satisfaction.

- **Self-discovery**: As individuals embark on a journey of self-discovery and self-awareness, emotional intelligence leads to elevated states of living and being.

- **Ethical living**: Practitioners are encouraged to live ethically and with compassion. When we can live in a "we" centered society rather than an "I" centered community the benefits to all around us are limitless.

- **Connection to Source**: Silva Mind Control fosters a connection to a higher source or divine energy. There is no stronger power that you can generate in yourself once you have complete faith in the source and yourself, it is the highest realm you can exist in.

- **Spiritual growth**: Continuous spiritual development and evolution are embraced. Spiritually, you can go from level to level, experiencing more and more inner peace, enhanced intuition, and awakened abilities.

- **The mindset of abundance**: By embracing abundance as a spiritual concept, you become a magnet to the positive energy which is then matched by the universe.

- **Surrender and trust**: Practicing surrender and trust in the spiritual journey releases you from fear and anger, and builds a level of confidence that is unmatched by anything else.

So now you can see the spiritual benefits and how they can lead to greater life satisfaction. But how do you get there? All this information is redundant unless you can begin a spiritual practice to ignite these levels of success.

Let's go on a journey to discover the Silva techniques you can incorporate into your daily schedule to activate inner peace.

INNER EXPLORATION AND SELF-DISCOVERY TECHNIQUES

Let's dive into some inner exploration and self-discovery techniques.

17 Self-Discovery Techniques to Support Your Spiritual Growth

Uncovering the Silva techniques that support your unique spiritual journey will help you in every aspect of your life. You don't have to choose one versus another, you can choose many, the most important thing is to commit to one practice regularly.

1. **Meditation:** Explore your inner thoughts and emotions. Begin with a short daily practice using the alpha deeper relaxation meditation to begin your journey. Meditation alone increases your self-awareness; you begin to see how your emotions and thoughts affect your behavior which helps you to change or modify your reactions to discover a different level of inner peace.

2. **Mindfulness**: Cultivate your present-moment awareness. This encourages you to pause more; to become the observer of your

verbal narrative. Do you have a running script of positive or negative thoughts in your mind? Mindfulness helps you to see and pinpoint where you can make changes to be more confident, joyful, and calmer in day-to-day living.

3. **Journaling**: Reflect on your thoughts and feelings and write them down. Now, this is key to unlocking many negative behaviors, plus it enables you to integrate pieces of yourself you may have avoided or abandoned. While this might seem time-consuming, journaling is a tool that helps you understand why you're feeling the way you do. It explains why you're behaving the way you are! It acts as a point of reflection, a measure to see how far you've come. And it works!

4. **Visualization:** Visualization helps uncover subconscious patterns. Through visualization, you can create images in your mind that become real. Imagine wanting to reach a goal like moving to a new city. Visualization is the tool that pushes you into taking action to do the necessary tasks to enable a move to the city. When we can feel the outcome of a successful scene, our brain desires it more and more and pulls us toward making it happen. It helps to destroy cognitive dissonance, the very thing that keeps you from your destined path.

5. **Self-reflection**: Self-reflection helps you understand your beliefs and behaviors so that you can become the person you want to be. Begin by listing the behaviors and habits of people you admire so you can emulate those personality traits; this helps you to get there faster.

6. **Dream analysis**: Interpret your subconscious messages through dreams. Dreams have hidden messages and are sometimes premonitions. Try and write your dreams down upon waking, so you can keep a diary to see how they affect your behavior and emotions.

7. **Shadow work**: Confront and integrate suppressed aspects of yourself through shadow work. The magic in you is in the work you're avoiding; this is the hidden secret of shadow work. Probably the ultimate resource for aligning you with your life's purpose, helping you become a complete and whole person. Confronting the pieces of yourself that you've hidden away deep within yourself, enables you to put the missing pieces of your puzzle together, and this is when the universe and abundance open up for you.

8. **Emotional release**: Process and release your repressed or stacked emotions. This helps to free yourself from stored pain and anger that can erupt into illness and poor health. Trapped emotions need to be released and integrated as part of the process of becoming whole.

9. **Personality assessments**: Gain insights into your personality traits. Find out why you have reactive behavior or why certain people trigger you. This is often because they mirror a quality you possess but are in deep denial of. Once you begin the road to accepting all parts of yourself, this is the time when you will slip into your life's purpose. You can simply start with journaling and noting down feelings you are experiencing, looking at why you are feeling them, and if there are any patterns in your behavior.

10. **Body awareness**: Connect with emotions and needs. You can start this by doing a body scan. There are many free online videos you can use to try a body scan. It's a simple way to feel each part of your body to see where there is tension, heaviness, pain, or stress; this helps you to identify it, focus on it, and eliminate it.

11. **Creative expression**: Tap into your unconscious insights. these may be revealed to you when you are under deeper exploration

of yourself. It's not uncommon for the activities and creative expression you had as a child to resurface as you begin to revert to your authentic self. This is a beyond joyful, fulfilling experience.

12. **Intuition development:** Cultivate inner guidance or intuition by unlocking your third eye. Remember, the magic inside you is in the work you are avoiding.

13. **Inner child work**: Heal and understand your inner child. This is never as easy as it seems, especially if you have experienced major trauma, and your inner child may be reluctant to come forward. Usually in the process of shadow work, your inner child will be reunited with you. Have patience, understand self-love, and know that the more care you give to yourself, the more this journey will unfold and push you toward alignment.

14. **Empathy and compassion**: Foster self-understanding. The understanding of yourself will help you in the understanding of all your relationships. All the complexities, the annoyances, the irritations and triggers you have with others, all stem from you. Once you unpick those, you will find a new level of relationship with yourself, your health, wealth, and also with everyone else from your lover to your co-worker, to your kids.

15. **Solitude and silence**: Solitude and silence will help facilitate inner exploration. This is where you can find stillness, calm, and inner peace. It's the place where it feels okay to be on your own; in fact, to be standing in your power. This place is a consistent journey for you to practice, with no destination.

16. **Retreats and nature immersion**: These can deepen self-journeys and fast-track any progress that you are making by working with collective energy. Nature immersion is fundamental for change and to stay grounded, especially when you are doing tough work, like inner child or shadow work. Grounding is imperative to keep

your spirit connected with the Earth, the giver of life, while your soul transcends to the multiverse for higher intelligence and guidance.

17. **Personal growth resources:** Utilize self-help materials. We are fortunate enough to have personal growth tools for free at our fingertips. Use them! Find out what you like and do more of it. The first step in this journey is making a schedule that you will stick to increase self-awareness, the rest will unfold as you become addicted to creating the best version of yourself!

CONNECTING WITH HIGHER CONSCIOUSNESS THROUGH MEDITATION

Think of meditation as a doorway, a doorway to a transformative spiritual experience. One where you will connect to a higher power, your higher consciousness. Once you've connected to your higher self, there's no turning back. You'll be able to dip into higher guidance almost immediately. It may take a while to get there but you can train yourself to slip into the alpha state whenever you want to especially with the 3 Fingers Technique.

Let's explore the ways that you can engage with your higher consciousness through meditation:

Stillness and Silence

Meditation allows connection through inner stillness. Inner stillness develops when you can quieten the mind and meditation provides the gateway for this. It may not happen straight away but observing what happens when you try to calm the mind shows you what needs working on. Say, for example, you begin to have intrusive thoughts, you can observe what comes up and begin the process to identify why that happens. All this leads to a higher version of yourself because you become so self-aware.

Silence helps you to connect with the present moment and the more you practice silence, the more you begin to appreciate it. It is a wonderful tool for heightening your awareness.

Higher Self-Exploration

Seek wisdom and guidance. This introspective journey will take you on a path to find what you want out of life. When you set an intention and begin to meditate, certain things will come up that give you a deeper understanding of your intention. During this moment of stillness, you can ask yourself questions and trust the answers, as they won't be included in external matters. The wisdom you are seeking is right inside of you, you simply need to tap into it.

Unity and Oneness

Feel connected to the universe. You can start by meditating with plants to feel their energy and establish your interconnectedness with all universal things. You can project yourself into the time-space continuum and transcend the past, present, and future if your spiritual journey takes you there. The unity and oneness that meditation provides are limitless, just like your journey and spiritual growth.

Intuitive Insights

Gaining higher conscious insights is relatively simple in meditation. Your mind becomes still and as you become the observer, you receive divine information or downloads. Meditation is similar to gardening, you spend a lot of time turning over the soil, preparing the ground for the new green shoots of life. Water it daily with your incremental practice, until one day the little green shoots poke through the soil, and keep on growing and growing into beautiful plants and new life. Imagine this is your intuitive insight; the more you practice, the more it will grow and develop.

Spiritual Growth

You can experience profound growth in your spirituality simply through sheer enjoyment of the practice itself. Learning to self-soothe and observe your mind, to achieve total peace of mind is an extraordinarily good place to be. Several things start to take shape when you connect with your higher consciousness. Self-realization becomes a new part of your life that encourages active changes in the way you behave. Your awareness becomes expanded, not only do you see yourself in a new light but you begin to observe others more closely. This can lead to a sense of not fitting in or choosing to not associate with certain people anymore. Both of these aspects can force the transcendence of your ego and hugely alter aspects of your personality, as your spiritual growth increases your humility does too.

Alignment With Purpose

A byproduct of this increased self-awareness brings you into the alignment of your life's purpose. Especially if you are meditating to release and integrate a lost piece of yourself that you previously considered to be shameful or hurtful. As soon as you start putting back together the person you were when you were born into this world, your path unfolds. You will begin to see that socialization and life's challenges knocked you off the path of your alignment and you do not know that this holds the key to your success and fulfillment.

Love & Compassion

Compassion is strengthened under your higher consciousness. You begin to see that others are not in the same place as you and forgiveness and elevated levels of understanding cultivate in your personality. This evolves into radiating love and compassion for humankind and leads to a much softer way of being and living.

Expanded Awareness

When you have access to higher realms, you begin to see the universe as limitless, which can be very freeing as you may have experienced such an insular existence before you began meditating. Harmony with nature and interconnectedness increases with all around you and you begin to see yourself in a deeper connection with all parts of the universe. Your level of understanding expands with complex issues being far easier to digest, all through this expanded awareness.

Integration in Daily Life

Connecting with your higher consciousness will influence your daily life positively. Life will not feel so tough, challenges will become puzzles you need to solve, relationships will grow and you will nurture the ones that are important to you. Your emotional intelligence will be more important to you, so with that, you will see changes within yourself. How you approach your relationship with everything, from your bank account to your neighbor's dog will become important. Understanding everything at a much deeper level will help you to work through challenges and you will view everything as a lesson or a teaching.

Gratitude and Reverence

When you start appreciating what you have, your life changes. When you begin to see that life is happening for you, not to you, you'll notice the challenges you face are part of the puzzle you need to solve to cultivate your purpose and message. You embrace a new desire to help others and make an impact in the world using the things you've struggled with, and you will be thankful for all these lessons. You have now awakened gratitude for everything that grows inside of you, and you will see in this higher state of consciousness, a version of yourself that vibrates at a higher level of intelligence.

Oneness With All Beings

We are all one. Just as following the spiritual path will lead to an expanded awareness it will also lead you to the realization of your interconnectedness with the universe. It will start with the same things around you such as plants and trees, animals, and the seasons. Then you will notice your interconnectedness with friends and family, relationships deepen and flow better. Then it spreads out into the world around you, your frequency is felt by people in the street, harmony is greater among strangers, and your awareness is heightened perhaps making you more vigilant. Oneness is experienced at all levels and in every situation, and when you are alone, meditate on your experience in the universe, allowing yourself to travel through the space-time continuum.

VISUALIZATION FOR PURPOSE AND MEANING

Visualization is the key that unlocks an idea in the real world; it transforms what you desire into something tangible. It is a hidden power that makes your desires so strong that you begin taking action to create your goal instantly.

So, how does this help with purpose and meaning? Well, when you visualize you are likely to choose something you desire from your heart space. You won't be asking for a new winter coat or a new set of pants, but you will be visualizing your heart's desires, such as a home, a holiday, or a new career. Perhaps these things seem a little out of reach and we don't know immediately how to attain them, so we visualize the big dreams and then once outside of meditation, we begin to see the baby steps that will get us there.

When it comes to purpose and meaning, and we meditate from a sacred place of truth and authenticity, what's hidden here is usually your life's purpose. The things that you're too scared to go and get or stop everything else to make room for. But in these quiet moments, you connect with that purpose, especially how it will feel when you are fulfilled by it. Your brain now knows that feeling and wants it more and more, faster and faster; and then it starts to unfold.

Interestingly, anyone who wants to change their life in any way is guided to visualization. It remains one of the most powerful tools in getting further and deeper into your spiritual development.

WRAP-UP AND ACTION STEPS

1. Doing shadow work is the key to unlocking the traumas that prevent you from growing spiritually and living the life of your dreams.

2. Meditation is a critical part of spiritual growth and has many benefits that all lead to greater emotional intelligence.

3. Growth does not have to be expensive, it simply requires the currency of scheduled time.

4. Your higher purpose or mission in life is the place where you will feel the most fulfillment.

5. Visualization is the key to going further and faster in your spiritual journey.

A spiritual high is usually the most fulfilling aspect of Silva Mind Control techniques but you're probably also wondering how to utilize all this good stuff to get ahead in your professional life.

Well, I just read your mind! So, let's jump to that next.

CHAPTER 10:
MIND CONTROL HACK #7:
UNLOCKING
PROFESSIONAL SUCCESS

When we're growing up there are all sorts of people telling us what to do when really what we need is space to work out who to be. –**Elliot Page**

When Silva Mind Control techniques were first used in a co-op for marketable inventions, Idea Bank Inc. Chicago, Richard Harrow, the owner, posted a marketing problem to see if Silva graduates could give practical answers, to an issue that took him 10 years to solve. He was blown away to find what took him 10 years, took the graduates only 10 minutes to work out!

SILVA MIND CONTROL FOR CAREER SUCCESS

Personal growth experts and the millionaire mindsets of the world's best entrepreneurs will both tell you emotional intelligence is worth far more than any skill or qualification you can acquire. By creating this resilient, can-do approach to just about anything, you become undefeatable. Couple that with the ability to get along with everyone, while maintaining a positive attitude, you will become the perfect employee or business owner.

Career Success Mindset

So, let's break it down and take a look at the mindset that could unlock your professional success.

- **Career goal setting**. It's easier to hit milestones, attract clients, and get a promotion when you can visualize how the outcome feels. Your brain will force you to get there even quicker than you anticipate.

- **Visualization** for success is the key to moving forward. You have to know and see where you want to go; feeling that emotion undoubtedly gets you there faster.

- **Confidence boosting** is one of those chicken and egg scenarios. You need more confidence to push ahead in your professional career and you get more confidence as you take the action steps to do it. Win-win!

- **Focus and concentration** improve when you can learn to be still. You will also have the added impact of seeing your goal come to fruition, so this will help you remain laser focused.

- **Overcoming obstacles** won't be a problem as you will no longer see them as obstacles, only challenges that you need to work through.

- **Stress management** is greatly reduced as you learn the value of pausing and breathing, watching your emotions rise and fall away, and staying mindful knowing that problems aren't there to attack you, they are just unmanaged situations.

- **A positive mindset** will make colleagues and clients both be attracted to you and this can only be a good thing, for your status within a company or your profit margin!

- **Improved decision-making**. Speed and clarity are renewed as you gain inner confidence and even if you make an incorrect decision, your ability to pivot and move to a different approach is enhanced. You won't care about making a wrong decision since you'll know that you can change direction at any time.

- **Networking and communication**. Maybe communication was awkward and uncomfortable before but now you are ready to listen, and people love to be heard. Networking will become fun and interesting.

- **Public speaking and presentation**. You'll also gain a renewed sense of confidence when speaking in public also because you won't be looking at your presentation from just your point of view. Your expanded awareness will help you embrace all sorts of different ideas and concepts making you an interesting and dynamic speaker.

- **Leadership and management** options both expand when you have an increased self-awareness and emotional intelligence. Others see you as a leader and you see yourself as a leader.

- **Time management** is improved when your self-care improves. And you will see that simply by spending time with yourself and connecting with a deeper part of your psyche, you will regain a new respect and appreciation of yourself. So much of the Silva Method involves increased self-awareness, you naturally find a new level of self-love and this translates into your having more respect and care with how you spend your time.

- **Creativity and problem**-solving are also advanced as your intuition allows you to tap into parts of yourself that you may have not been able to access before. When we drop social barriers and expectations of ourselves, we open up to more possibilities.

Such as visions, dreams, and hopes we had as a child, and we see that anything is possible, and we find that we can create anything we want.

- **Negotiation skills** are improved because your level of empathy expands. When you can see others' side of the argument or point of view, negotiating becomes fair and benefits both parties. We begin to make harmonious agreements, work as part of a team with work we enjoy, and earn the respect of our co-workers in the process.

- **Career progression** is revitalized, especially from the visualization you practice. When you can see yourself in a new role or at a new level of progression; when you can hear and feel how that emotion embraces you, it is easier to reach your goals and dreams.

- **Emotional intelligence** of advanced levels is reached when you simply become more self-aware. This is the beautiful byproduct of the Silva Method. You don't need to practice emotional intelligence, it just happens from the inner work you start putting in. And it will become your most valuable asset.

- **Adaptability and resilience** are other strengths that keep on growing and add to your professional success. You won't be so bothered by the things people say about you. You will face any challenge like it is a gift, there to teach you a lesson. You become fearless in the face of opposition because you will be solution-focused, which helps to destroy stress and anxiety.

- **Continuous learning** is the path that expands alongside your mind. When you can see and feel that your capabilities are endless, you become a sponge, without even trying, looking for ways to increase your emotional intelligence and powers.

- **Work-life balance** no longer is a problem. You embrace the full benefit of having time off to rest and restore, knowing that your creativity level is elevated once you've replenished your mind and body. Another beautiful byproduct of this is your close relationships are enhanced as a consequence of spending more time with your loved ones, and not stressing about work.

SETTING AND ACHIEVING GOALS

Setting and achieving goals becomes easier once you start using some of the Silva techniques such as visualization on your mental screen or the dynamic meditation. You won't believe how you can take your professional achievements to the next level by accessing these powerful tools.

If you're not sure how to start, here's a comprehensive guide that will help you get on track and keep you accountable to reach your aspirations:

- **Goal Clarity**: Clearly define your professional goals, up to 3 at a time is a good, manageable number of goals to use in your visualization. Any more than that would feel less achievable.

- **Visualization**: Visualize yourself achieving these goals. Feel the emotions that would be generated when you reach these goals. Tap into that version of yourself, how you would look, and how you would behave; this will encourage your brain to get there faster.

- **Action planning**: Develop step-by-step plans to attain them. Don't go any further than 3 months in the future and that way you'll find the smaller, more achievable steps easy to do, and recognize signs and symbols of your goals when they present themselves to you in your daily life.

- **Goal prioritization**: Rank goals by importance and timeline. Make a planner for up to 3 years, but break down your goals into subsections so they are attainable. Start with weekly goals, then monthly goals, move to quarterly goals, then yearly goals.

- **Goal monitoring**: Regularly track progress toward goals. Keep a journal so you can measure your progress, what went well, what didn't go so well, and how far you've come. Reflection is a powerful tool for fast-tracking success.

- **Time management**: Allocate time effectively for goal pursuits. Increased self-awareness brings greater self-respect and a renewed appreciation of your energy and resources. One of those is your time. You will learn automatically how precious your time is, so begin to change how you allocate it. Nothing is more important than the time spent working on yourself.

- **Overcoming obstacles**: Use problem-solving skills to overcome challenges. Dynamic meditation is one of the key Silva problem-solving techniques. See the outcome and you will find the pieces of the puzzle to get you there. New ideas will present themselves to you through this technique.

- **Positive mindset**: Cultivate optimism and self-belief in goal attainment. Make affirmations to support your goals and courage. Repeat them three times a day. Learn to believe in yourself, and don't expect it to come automatically. You have to work at it.

- **Accountability**: Hold yourself accountable for goal progress. Use your journal as a measure of progress. Don't beat yourself up when you don't reach a goal on time, simply look at what you could have done better and praise yourself for the learning.

- **Celebrate milestones**: Acknowledge and celebrate achievements. Celebrations, however small, are the key to keeping going. We all love the feeling of treating ourselves so do it regularly. Take yourself out for a coffee and a slice of cake and be with yourself in a celebratory moment.

- **Adaptability**: Be flexible and adjust goals when needed. You are the master of your ship, you get to determine when you achieve a goal so if something needs changing, stay in control and be proud of yourself for making the necessary adjustments.

- **Motivation techniques**: Use motivation strategies to stay on track. These can vary from journaling to affirmations to meditation. Pick what you enjoy and connect with the source that keeps you moving.

- **Seek support**: Seek guidance and support from mentors or peers. There are endless free resources online or connect with a coach or mentor who will push you or help you resolve a block or obstacle.

- **Persistence**: Persevere in the face of setbacks or delays. These are happening for you not to you; you never know what is on the other side of a problem so don't feel defeated, this may be happening in your best interest.

- **Break goals into steps**: Divide big goals into smaller achievable tasks. These will feel doable and you can then celebrate when you have reached the outcome. This is pure motivation to keep going.

- **Visualize success**: Use visualization to reinforce success. Create it in your head first, see it, feel it and you'll want it more. You'll also be inadvertently training your brain to get there faster.

- **Reward yourself**: Celebrate milestones with rewards. This has a compound effect of releasing positive energy while reinforcing motivation. Always celebrate your wins!

- **Daily affirmations**: Use positive affirmations to stay focused. These are reminders of who you are or who you want to be, they are vital to keeping a positive script running in your head.

- **Learn from setbacks**: Embrace setbacks as learning opportunities. Setbacks happen for a reason> Maybe you don't know enough yet, or maybe there is something else to add to the problem. Whatever it is think of it as a gift. A gift of time and clarity.

- **Continuous improvement**: Always strive for personal and professional growth. And, if you use the Silva Method techniques, your meditation progress will keep you interested in wanting to know more and create even greater expansion. Your continuous improvement is limitless.

VISUALIZATION FOR PROBLEM-SOLVING

When you can see the problem clearly and the outcome you desire, visualization for problem-solving is a breeze. Use the dynamic meditation method to see the future resolution and you'll soon be problem-solving. Snapping into your subconscious to solve a problem will become your new normal.

Visualization for Problem-Solving Steps

Here are the steps to follow to solve work-related problems:

1. Relax and clear your mind by getting into the alpha state. Use the 3 Fingers Technique to get there immediately (refer to chapter 3).

2. Through dynamic meditation, visualize the problem and explore possible solutions.

3. Envision a positive resolution using the Silva dynamic meditation technique to solve work-related problems or issues.

4. Choose a real problem you face, one that hasn't resolved itself yet.

5. Pull up your mental screen.

6. Create the problem on the screen so you can see it.

7. Now gently push this scene off to the right.

8. From the left, slide onto the screen another scene that will take place in the future where everything begins to resolve.

9. Then push this screen off to the right and replace it with another from the left that has your defined, positive, and desired outcome.

10. Immerse yourself in this outcome. See, hear, feel, and embrace the emotion associated with these results. Make it so vivid that it feels real and stay with it make it until you get the full immersion of the sensation.

11. Now at the count of 5, you will be wide awake and feeling better than before.

WRAP-UP AND ACTION STEPS

1. Your mindset is the key to professional success.

2. Use the dynamic meditation and 3 Mental Screen technique to solve any professional-related problem.

3. Visualization is a key part of problem solving.

4. Problem solving will be your "magic" skill and will help you troubleshoot any issue or emergency at work.

5. Unlocking professional success will give you a consistently positive attitude.

6. It will help you build inner peace and confidence and eliminate your constant state of stress at work.

7. The key to your professional success is in your energy and beliefs.

Now I know you must be so excited to start your Silva Method practices to slay your professional life! But I'm sure you also have a nagging doubt in the back of your mind that says "Ok that's work, But how about my personal life ?" "What if things don't go my way personally? What can I do?" Well, I'm about to show you. Let's keep going.

CHAPTER 11: MIND CONTROL HACK #8: PERSONAL SUCCESS AND YOU

Recognizing that you are not where you want to be is a starting point to begin changing your life. –**Deborah Day**

It's not uncommon to not know what you want in life. Some would even say that knowing what you want is one of life's mysteries. So, if you're using a process of elimination until now, that's okay. Most of us will take any job to see if we like it. Most of us will date various partners to find who we're attracted to. Most of us will put up with an unsatisfactory life until we get so fed up with it that we demand change.

But what if I told you there was a better way than living your life on auto pilot and to know exactly what you want and when you want it? Have I got your attention?

You cannot nail every goal in life. Some things will not work out for a good reason, and you'll be grateful they didn't. However, you can become an expert in utilizing Silva's tools to maximize your chances for success by zeroing in on it and nailing it. And through your success, you can help others do it too.

Here are some compelling testimonies of users of the Silva Method, taken from Joyful Journey, (2023). The first is a cancer patient who found incredible strength using the Silva Method in their pain journey:

> "When I was sick with cancer and on treatment I would use the Long Relax for total and healing relaxation, adding the Pain Control Technique to minimize the pain. The results were terrific. I was told I was a model patient at the hospital. I now use the techniques mostly on the road to have an uneventful journey and to be moving the traffic along: I set duration for my travel and using the techniques always find that I achieve my goal, arriving safely, relaxed, and on time. I use the sleep technique whenever I'm restless to have good quality sleep. Also, I sometimes have to travel long distances to attend meetings so, when I know I'm going to have a very short night's sleep I use the Long Relax to improve the quality of sleep to be alert whilst driving and during the meeting."

The next is something we all can relate to, reactive behavior. Just look at the results!

> "I used to get uptight quite easily but since I have taken the Silva Course I have found myself far more relaxed and at work, my colleagues who would know me to lose my temper, are surprised as I don't anymore! Overall the days flow more easily."

And lastly, the undeniable synchronicities of using enhanced intuition.

> "My Mum was trying to contact my brother in London but none of us knew where to reach him. So I used my Three Fingers Technique and there he was in the middle of London, in front of my car; and just at that time, the traffic lights turned red which gave us time for him to come to my door and give me his phone number!"

Testimonies are always encouraging, but these are simply mind-blowing and encourage us to know that anything we desire is possible.

SILVA MIND CONTROL FOR PERSONAL SUCCESS

In their personal lives some people will be looking for a life partner, getting over an addiction, finding a new job or getting a raise. The Silva Method can help you with all of these personal problems or issues.

Mind Control: Personal success can be attained by using Silva's meditation practices. Just through reaching the alpha state you can achieve this, even without moving forward into the dynamic meditation. That's how powerful meditation really is! Refer to chapter 3 for a refresher on these key practices.

Problem-solving: Effective problem-solving is crucial in life and can be applied not only to professional issues but to personal ones as well. Silva's dynamic meditation can help you master problem solving. Once you've mastered this, problems disappear and challenges become easy to solve and instead of creating barriers, it becomes more like putting pieces of a puzzle together.

Consistency: Consistency is key when using the Silva practices. So do it twice a day. Try doing the meditation in the morning and before bed. That is the ideal time.

Self-discipline: When you become organized and accountable make these practices part of your life and schedule, literally anything is possible.

The Silva Mind Control method practices can lead you to personal success through:

- improved focus
- goal setting

- confidence

- stress reduction

- enhanced creativity

- positive affirmations

- improved memory

- mind-body connection

- increased intuition

- alignment with the law of attraction

Your success depends on dedication, consistency, and the extent of your belief in the Silva techniques. Always approach them with an open mind, critical thinking, and above all an open heart, ready to learn and receive.

BOUNCING BACK FROM FAILURE

First things first, there is no such thing as failure. Many challenges require solutions and lessons to learn. How you frame failure in your mind will shape exactly how you behave. This will have a direct effect on your psyche and impact on your limitations. Do you want to feel limited or limitless? That's the question you need to ask yourself. If it's the latter, then failure does not exist, and you can learn how to realistically deal with that concept by using the following guidelines:

1. **Accept and acknowledge**: Acknowledge the failure and accept that setbacks are a natural part of life. Avoid denying or suppressing the emotions associated with failure.

2. **Analyze and learn**: Reflect on the "failure" to understand what went wrong and why. Identify lessons learned and areas for improvement.

3. **Maintain perspective**: Put the failure into perspective. Remind yourself of past successes and realize that one failure doesn't define your entire life or abilities.

4. **Positive self-talk**: Replace negative self-talk with positive and encouraging statements. Be kind to yourself and avoid dwelling on self-blame.

5. **Seek support**: Reach out to friends, family, or mentors for support and encouragement. Talking to others can provide valuable insights and help you see things from different angles.

6. **Set new goals**: Establish new, realistic goals that align with your aspirations. Break them down into smaller, achievable steps to build momentum.

7. **Take action**: Act on your new goals and plans. Take small steps to regain confidence and a sense of control over your life.

8. **Embrace resilience**: Cultivate resilience and a growth mindset. View failure as an opportunity for learning and growth rather than a dead-end.

9. **Learn from role models**: Read about or connect with individuals who have overcome failures to find inspiration and motivation.

10. **Adapt and persist**: Be willing to adapt your approach and persevere. Failure is often a stepping stone to success.

11. **Celebrate progress**: Acknowledge and celebrate every small achievement along the way. It will boost your morale and keep you motivated.

12. **Practice self-care**: Take care of your physical and mental well-being. Engage in activities that bring you joy and help reduce stress.

13. **Stay optimistic**: Cultivate optimism and a positive outlook on the future. Visualize success and believe in your abilities.

14. **Stay persistent**: Don't let fear of failure prevent you from trying again. Persistence and determination are crucial to overcoming setbacks.

CONTINUED GROWTH WITH SILVA MIND CONTROL

The more you practice with Silva you realize there are no limits to your growth. You find that there is no final destination either, simply continued expansion that will impact every corner of your life.

Here's how to stay focused:

- **Consistent practice**: Make a habit of daily meditation and visualization exercises. Consistency is key to strengthening your mind and achieving lasting results.

- **Set evolving goals**: Continuously set new and evolving goals for yourself. As you achieve one goal, replace it with another to maintain a sense of purpose and direction.

- **Review and refine**: Regularly review your progress and experiences with Silva Mind Control. Identify areas where you can improve and refine your techniques.

- **Expand knowledge**: Continue learning about the mind, consciousness, and personal development. Read books, attend workshops, or engage in discussions to expand your knowledge.

- **Join a community**: Connect with like-minded individuals who also practice Silva Mind Control. Being part of a supportive community can provide motivation and encouragement.

- **Overcome challenges**: Use the techniques to overcome problems, challenges and obstacles in your life. Apply the lessons learned from failure and setbacks to grow stronger.

- **Visualize success**: Keep visualizing your desired outcomes and success. This mental rehearsal can help reinforce your beliefs and attract positive experiences.

- **Gratitude practice**: Cultivate a gratitude practice to focus on the positives in your life. Expressing gratitude can enhance your overall well-being and attract more positive experiences.

- **Expand your limits**: Use Silva Mind Control to push beyond your perceived limits. Explore new opportunities and step outside your comfort zone.

- **Adapt techniques**: Tailor the Silva techniques to suit your specific needs and preferences. Experiment with different approaches to find what works best for you.

- **Teach others**: Share your knowledge and experiences with others. Teaching can deepen your understanding and reinforce your practice.

- **Stay patient**: Personal growth is a continuous journey, and it takes time and patience. Stay committed to the process and be kind to yourself along the way.

- **Track your progress**: Keep a journal to record your experiences, insights, and achievements. Tracking your progress can provide motivation and remind you of how far you've come.

- **Apply mindfulness**: Practice mindfulness in your everyday life. Be fully present in each moment and bring your newfound awareness into your daily activities.

Visualization for Problem Solving Steps

Here are the steps to follow to solve personal problems:

1. Breathe deeply through the nose and exhale through the mouth.

2. Relax and clear your mind by getting into the alpha state. Use the 3 Fingers Technique to get there immediately (refer to chapter 3).

3. Through dynamic meditation, visualize the problem eg. finding a job and explore possible solutions.

4. Envision a positive resolution using the Silva dynamic meditation technique to solve personal problems or issues.

5. Choose a real problem you face, one that hasn't resolved itself yet.

6. Pull up your mental screen.

7. Create the problem on the screen so you can see it.

8. Now gently push this scene off to the right.

9. From the left, slide onto the screen another scene that will take place in the future where everything begins to resolve.

10. Then push this screen off to the right and replace it with another from the left that has your defined, positive, and desired outcome.

11. Immerse yourself in this outcome. See, hear, feel, and embrace the emotion associated with these results. Make it so vivid that it feels real and stay with it make it until you get the full immersion of the sensation.

12. Now at the count of 5, you will be wide awake and feeling better than before.

WRAP-UP AND ACTION STEPS

1. Silva Mind Control can also be used to resolve personal problems whether it be finding a partner, overcoming an addiction, or finding a new job.

2. Framing how you view failure will be key in becoming successful since persistence is the name of the game. Is there such a thing as failure after all?

3. The byproduct of practicing meditation will kick start every corner of success building in your life, by providing you with confidence and new insights to solve your problems whether it's finding a new job, dealing with an addiction, a complicated family relationship, or finding a partner.

4. As a result of your alpha meditation practice, you will have access to enhanced intuition will make you more creative in the pursuit of solving your problems.

5. Enhanced creativity will connect you with your higher consciousness as well as higher intelligence.

6. Your higher consciousness will connect you with not only to the solution to your specific issue but also eventually to life's purpose.

7. To harness the power of the Silva practice to help you with your personal problems, follow the steps for the *Visualization for Problem Solving Step*s.

8. Et voila!

|CONCLUSION

As we approach the end of our journey together, so much has been activated inside of you! What do you feel was the turning point for you on this road to higher intelligence and expanded intuition?

Although the alpha state is not so far from the beta state, it makes a huge difference of how we think and behave from this new place of creativity and deep relaxation within us.

Specifically, how has your life changed? Have you tried accessing the alpha state in the morning, and the evening, as José Silva suggested? If you haven't, then make sure that you try this meditation at least once a day because the benefits and results you will experience will be nothing short of miraculous, even from day one!

Isn't it incredible to think that so much more of the world is now open to you? Your mind is now like the world, huge and expansive, and as deep as the ocean with no end in sight. You are now able to create from a place where everything and nothing exists.

What is your relationship with money now like? Do you have a renewed sense of respect for the coins and notes in your purse or wallet? Do you think twice before throwing food out or getting rid of clothes instead of recycling them? I hope that you have activated this part of the Law of Attraction because just as some people remain poor, others become wealthy by practicing the Silva techniques. The universe is unbiased, and your energy behaves like a magnet.

One of the most remarkable things about the Silva Method is the self-healing that can be activated just through thought alone. We know that worries, stress, and trauma can cause huge mental instabilities with effects that move through our physical body, causing disease.

Isn't it empowering to know that just through the use of the mind we can heal the things that we create? What will you heal, or prevent, now?

Are you excited about creating deeper levels of intimacy with your partner? The level of intimacy described in the book has such a beautiful quality. It's almost like a secret place for you and your partner to go to any time you want. Something that's just shared between the two of you, which in itself is incredibly intimate. I hope that you will practice this technique.

I wonder if, like me, when first learning the Silva Method, you tried to find something that you thought you'd lost? How is your memory recall now? Have you activated the Three Fingers Technique?

Now that we are reaching the end of our journey together, look how far you've come emotionally, how much you've grown. I'm sure that now when others are speaking, you are listening more. I bet you're pausing before you answer to think about the effect of your words. When you have negative thoughts, you're now substituting them with positive affirmations and statements.

This Silva program encompasses so many aspects of your mental and physical well-being. There is no corner of your life that this doesn't impact and that makes the Silva Method a very special and unique practice indeed.

Before we go, I want to remind you again about Helene Hadsell's story. This woman created win after win in her life through the use of the Silva method. She created for herself a life of comfort with a whole lot of fun, and got to turn her story into a very powerful message. There is nothing you cannot achieve with the power of your mind!

What will your message be moving forward? How will you make the Silva Method work for you?

Because ultimately, all you have to do is decide what you want from life.

Activate your alpha state, see it, feel it, and get out there and experience it!

Isn't living the life that you choose, by your rules, with success, inner peace, and abundance, the life you always dreamt of? When it comes to Silva Mind Control, the world is your oyster; so, get out there and get it!

Free Goodwill

"The mind is not a vessel to be filled, but a fire to be kindled." – Plutarch

Thank you for completing the transformative journey delving into the power of your subconscious mind to guide you onto a new growth path, revealing opportunities you may never have thought possible until now! With this workbook, you now have all the tools, secrets, and resources to LIVE YOUR IDEAL LIFE! it's time to pass on your newfound knowledge and show other readers where they can find the same help.

The power of the subconscious mind and the Silva Mind Control method is kept alive when we pass on our knowledge – and you're helping ME to do just that. Our mission is *to make SILVA MIND CONTROL accessible to everyone*. Everything we do stems from that mission. And, the only way for us to accomplish that mission is by reaching... well...*everyone*.

This is where you come in. Most people do, in fact, judge a book by its cover (and its reviews). So here's my ask on behalf of a struggling individual entrepreneur growth seeker you've never met:

Simply by leaving your honest opinion of this book on Amazon, you'll show other individual growth-minded entrepreneurs where they can find the information they've been looking for to transform and live their best lives. You will be passing along the torch of THE POWER OF THE SUBCONSCIOUS MIND.

Your gift costs no money and less than 60 seconds to make real but can change your fellow growth seeker's life forever. Your review could help…

…one more small business provide for their community.

…one more entrepreneur support their family.

…one more employee get meaningful work.

…one more client transform their life.

…one more dream come true.

To get that 'feel good' feeling and help this person for real, all you have to do is…and it takes less than 60 seconds…leave a review. Simply scan the QR code below or visit https://www.amazon.com/review/review-your-purchases/?asin= B0CSB6DQJN to leave your review

Scan this QR code now

Review 8 Silva Hacks

If you feel good about helping a growth seeker like yourself, you are my kind of person! Welcome to the 8 Silva Mind Control Hacks community dedicated to positive change and growth. You're now one of us.

I'm excited to have helped you live your ideal life! Thank you from the bottom of my heart.

- Your biggest fan, Anabelle

Anabelle sl

PS - Fun fact: If you provide something of value to another person, it makes you more valuable to them. If you'd like goodwill straight from another individual like yourself seeking personal growth - and you believe this book will help them - send this book their way.

REFERENCES

Daniels, L. (2023). *The Silva Mind Control Method Workbook*.

Silva, J. (2022). *Silva Mind Control Method*. Gallery Books. (Original work published 1991)

International, O. (2015, July 29). *OSHO Dynamic Meditation – a revolution in consciousness*. www.youtube.com/watch?v=sbfVcigkNao&t=1098s

LeBoeuf, R. (2022, June 24). *50 best personal growth quotes*. www.snhu. edu/about-us/newsroom/education/personal-growth-quotes

Meditate and grow rich - how visualisation helped Helene Hadsell win every contest she entered (SPEC METHOD). (2017, October 14). path2inspiration. com/blogs/news/meditate-and-grow-rich-how-visualisation-helped-helene-hadsell-win-every-contest-she-entered-spec-method

Mindvalley. (2021, January 16). *20-minute Silva Centering exercise with Vishen Lakhiani*. www.youtube.com/watch?v=h_4GDXWBPCk

Silva Method testimonials. (n.d.). www.joyful-journey.net/offerings/silva-method/testimonials.html#:~:text=It%20has%20turned%20out%20to

Silva, J. (n.d.). *Guided to a lottery ticket*. Psychorientologist José Silva. https://José silva.net/guided-to-a-lottery-ticket/

Silva, J. (1999). *Silva Centering exercise | PDF*. https://www.scribd.com/doc/206448927/6663309-Silva-Centering-Exercise

Silva, J. (2022, November 20). *Silva three finger technique - a way to success*. https://silvamethod.com/stores/silva-three-fingers-technique-a-way-to-success/

Silva, L. (n.d.). *Manifest like a millionaire*. Laura Silva Quesada. https://laurasilvaquesada.com/manifest-like-a-millionaire

Silva, L. (2015, November 5). *Try this insomnia exercise that really works*. www.healyourlife.com/try-this-insomnia-exercise-that-really-works

Printed in Great Britain
by Amazon

56967429R00086